THE WORLD IN 2020

Towards a New Global Age

ORGANISATION FOR ECONOMIC CO-OPERATION AND DEVELOPMENT

ORGANISATION FOR ECONOMIC CO-OPERATION AND DEVELOPMENT

Pursuant to Article 1 of the Convention signed in Paris on 14th December 1960, and which came into force on 30th September 1961, the Organisation for Economic Co-operation and Development (OECD) shall promote policies designed:

- to achieve the highest sustainable economic growth and employment and a rising standard of living in Member countries, while maintaining financial stability, and thus to contribute to the development of the world economy;
- to contribute to sound economic expansion in Member as well as non-member countries in the process of economic development; and
- to contribute to the expansion of world trade on a multilateral, non-discriminatory basis in accordance with international obligations.

The original Member countries of the OECD are Austria, Belgium, Canada, Denmark, France, Germany, Greece, Iceland, Ireland, Italy, Luxembourg, the Netherlands, Norway, Portugal, Spain, Sweden, Switzerland, Turkey, the United Kingdom and the United States. The following countries became Members subsequently through accession at the dates indicated hereafter: Japan (28th April 1964), Finland (28th January 1969), Australia (7th June 1971), New Zealand (29th May 1973), Mexico (18th May 1994), the Czech Republic (21st December 1995), Hungary (7th May 1996), Poland (22nd November 1996) and the Republic of Korea (12th December 1996). The Commission of the European Communities takes part in the work of the OECD (Article 13 of the OECD Convention).

Publié en français sous le titre :

LE MONDE EN 2020
Vers une nouvelle ère mondiale

Reprinted 1997

ACKNOWLEDGEMENTS

This report sets out some of the key economic and social policy challenges for realising a "New Global Age". As such, it has required a broad, interdisciplinary team, with contributions from all parts of the OECD Secretariat.

Makoto Taniguchi initiated and assumed an oversight role for this project as Deputy Secretary-General until the end of 1996 and as Special Adviser to the Secretary-General until the end of May 1997. John West provided valuable assistance throughout this period and contributed greatly to the completion of the study after Makoto Taniguchi's departure. Friedrich Klau made an important contribution in the final stages of editing the report for publication.

Analytical work was coordinated by a team of experts in the OECD Development Centre consisting of Olivier Bouin, David O'Connor and David Turnham, with research assistance provided by Christophe Compainville. Contributions were made from OECD Directorates and Agencies as follows: Economics Department (Robert Ford, Pete Richardson and the staff of the International Trade and Investment Division); Environment Directorate (Eva Rosinger, Brendan Gillespie and Chris Chung); Development Co-operation Directorate (Richard Carey); Trade Directorate (Raed Safadi); Directorate for Financial, Fiscal and Enterprise Affairs (Rinaldo Pecchioli, Jeffrey Owens and Jan Schuijer); Directorate for Science, Technology and Industry (Jean-Eric Aubert, Mark Cantley and Wolfgang Hübner); Directorate for Education, Employment, Labour and Social Affairs (John Martin, Jean-Pierre Garson, Raymond Torres and Peter Hicks); Directorate for Food, Agriculture and Fisheries (Herbert Raidl and Josef Schmidhuber); Territorial Development Service (Josef Konvitz); Liaison and Co-ordination Unit (Hidehiro Iwaki); Advisory Unit on Multidisciplinary Issues (Barrie Stevens); International Energy Agency (Kenneth Wigley); Nuclear Energy Agency (Philippe Savelli); and the Club du Sahel (Roy Stacy).

Modelling work was undertaken by Dominique van der Mensbrugghe of the OECD Development Centre using the LINKAGE general equilibrium model. The Netherlands Bureau for Economic Policy Analysis made important contributions to the modelling work through adaptation of its WORLDSCAN model.

This project was supported by extra-budgetary funds contributed by the governments of Austria, Canada, Japan, the Netherlands and Norway.

TABLE OF CONTENTS

PREFACE

By Donald J. Johnston, Secretary-General of the OECD

The economic environment is changing rapidly. Globalisation is being increasingly driven by dynamic and emerging non-OECD economies, especially from Asia and Latin America. And the "Big Five" of Brazil, China, India, Indonesia and Russia are already playing important roles in many global issues – not only in trade and investment, but agriculture, energy (including nuclear) and the environment. We stand on the threshold of a "New Global Age", where all societies have the potential of participating actively in the world economy; where the benefits of liberalised world trade and investment could flow to all people; where the misery and poverty of much of the developing world could become a closed chapter of sad history, no longer a reality of the present.

This publication sets out a vision of the world economy in the year 2020 where governments and societies seize the challenge of realising a new age of global prosperity. This will not materialise automatically. It will require bold action by governments within and outside the OECD area to complete the borderless world through free flows of goods and services, capital and technology, to ensure high and equitable growth supported by stable and sustainable macroeconomic conditions and wide-ranging structural reforms. The importance of these conditions has been particularly highlighted in recent years by episodes of financial market instability in, for example, Southeast Asia and Latin America.

While a "New Global Age" promises improved quality of life the world over, innovative public policy responses and broad commitment will be required to reduce the risk that some groups within countries (including the most advanced), or even whole societies, are left behind. The potential for reducing poverty has never been so great. Failing to rise to this challenge should not be contemplated.

Economic expansion of the kind envisaged by the "New Global Age" will reap the benefits foreseen only if pursued within the context of environmental sustainability. There is an urgent need to deal effectively with issues such as greenhouse gas emissions, hazardous waste production, megacity evolution, intensification of agriculture, timber and fisheries exploitation, and demands on fresh water. International co-operation and vigorous action globally, regionally, nationally and locally are paramount. The means must be found to delink economic growth from the increasing environmental pressures which accompany it.

There is reason for optimism. As the century draws to a close, we are witnessing an astonishing acceleration in the pace of technological innovation. History has shown that necessity spawns invention; and that solutions often come from the least expected directions. While it is not possible to forecast which particular technological advances will provide solutions for our most pressing problems, there is much that can be done to stimulate innovation. Public policy can and should play a major role.

The window of opportunity to move globally toward an improved quality of life for all is now open. The challenge facing governments is to design and implement balanced policies which foster economic growth, protect the environment and ensure social justice. Unprecedented political will is needed. So, too, is the rigorous analysis of policy impacts, especially for policies whose underpinnings must combine the knowledge of many disciplines. These are major priorities for the OECD. Through interdisciplinary work across the full range of economic, social, environmental and developmental issues; through expanding and deepening interactions with non-OECD economies; through policy dialogues to build convergence in thinking and coordination in action, the OECD is making its contribution to realising the opportunities of the New Global Age.

In the world of tomorrow, we do not wish to live in a world divided by ideology as during the cold war, nor in a world divided by wealth and poverty as we see it today. In the present generation, we have a choice. We may choose to work together for the benefit of all, giving renewed meaning to the poem of Frank Scott which begins: "The world is my country, the human race is my race".

Donald J. Johnston
November 17, 1997.

KEY TO ABBREVIATIONS

AFTA	ASEAN Free Trade Area
AIJ	Activities Implemented Jointly
Annex I	Annex I countries refer to OECD Member countries, the CEECs, the Baltic republics, Belarus, the Russian Federation, and Ukraine, as signatories to the Framework Convention on Climate Change
APEC	Asian-Pacific Economic Co-operation
ASEAN	Association of Southeast Asian Nations, comprising Brunei, Indonesia, Malaysia, the Philippines, Singapore, Thailand and (since 1995) Vietnam
Big Five	Five large emerging economies – Brazil, China (including Hong Kong), India, Indonesia, and Russia (or sometimes the NIS)
Billion	Equivalent to 1 000 million
CEEC	Central and eastern European countries
CER	Australia New Zealand Closer Economic Relations Trade Agreement
CFC	Chlorofluorocarbon – chemical responsible for ozone depletion, and one of the GHG.
COP	Conference of the Parties
DAC	OECD Development Assistance Committee
DAE	Dynamic Asian Economies, comprising Chinese Taipei, Hong Kong, Malaysia, Republic of Korea, Singapore and Thailand
DAFFE	OECD Directorate for Financial, Fiscal and Enterprise Affairs
DSTI	OECD Directorate for Science, Technology and Industry
EBRD	European Bank for Reconstruction and Development
ECO	OECD Economics Department
EFTA	European Free Trade Area
ELSA	OECD Directorate for Education, Employment, Labour and Social Affairs
EMU	European Monetary Union
EU	European Union
FAO	Food and Agriculture Organisation
FCCC	Framework Convention on Climate Change. Convention signed at the Rio Earth Summit, June, 1992. Ratified by Annex I countries in March, 1994
FDI	Foreign direct investment
FTZ	Free Trade Zone
G7	Group of 7 leading industrialised countries: Canada, France, Germany, Italy, Japan, United Kingdom and the United States
GATS	General Agreement on Trade in Services
GATT	General Agreement on Tariffs and Trade (replaced by the WTO in 1995)
GDP	Gross domestic product (definition of national income)
GE	General equilibrium
GFCF	Gross Fixed Capital Formation
GHG	Greenhouse gas, any gas in the atmosphere that absorbs infrared radiation – dominated by carbon dioxide, but includes methane, CFCs, etc.
GII	Global information infrastructure
GTAP	Global Trade Analysis Program. GTAP is the source of most of the data used in the quantitative analysis, and is an international consortium of economists.

GW	Gigawatts. Unit of electrical energy equivalent to 10^9 watts, or 1 000 megawatts.
HG	High growth (scenario)
IEA	International Energy Agency
IFPRI	International Food Policy Research Institute
IITA	International Institute of Tropical Agriculture
ILO	International Labour Organisation
ILRI	International Livestock Research Institute
IMF	International Monetary Fund
IPCC	Intergovernmental Panel on Climate Change
IPR	Intellectual Property Rights
IT	Information technologies
MAI	Multilateral Agreement on Investment
MEA	Multilateral environment agreements
Mercosur	Common market formed by Argentina, Brazil, Paraguay and Uruguay
MFA	Multi-fibre Arrangement
MFN	Most favoured nation treatment
MRA	Mutual Recognition Agreements
Mt	Million tonnes
NAALC	North American Agreement on Labor Co-operation
NAFTA	North American Free Trade Agreement
NIS	Newly Independent States (of the former Soviet Union)
NME	Non-Member Economies or Non-OECD Economies
NMP	Net material product (definition of national output in centrally planned economies)
ODA	Official development assistance
OECD	Organisation for Economic Co-operation and Development
Ppmv	Parts per million by volume (measure of atmospheric concentration)
PPP	Purchasing Power Parities are the rate of currency conversion which eliminates the differences in price levels between countries. This means that a given sum of money, when converted into different currencies at these rates, will buy the same basket of goods and services in all countries.
R&D	Research and development
ROW	Rest of the World
SSA	Sub-Saharan Africa
TBT	Agreement on Technical Barriers to Trade
TFP	Total factor productivity
TNC	Transnational corporations
Trillion	Equivalent to 1 000 billion.
TRIMS	Agreement on Trade-related Investment Measures
TRIPS	Agreement on Trade-related Aspects of Intellectual Property Rights
UN	United Nations
UNCED	United Nations Conference on Environment and Development
UNCTAD	United Nations Conference on Trade and Development
UNCTC	United Nations Centre on Transnational Corporations
UNEP	United Nations Environment Programme
UR	Uruguay Round, recently concluded multilateral agreement for a reduction in trade barriers
WTO	World Trade Organisation

POLICY OVERVIEW

I. A WINDOW OF OPPORTUNITY

Global political and economic developments provide...

Over the past decade or so, a number of factors have profoundly changed the outlook for global political and economic developments: the increasingly widespread acceptance of democratic institutions and market-based economic development; rapid economic growth of several non-OECD economies, especially in the Asia-Pacific region; the emergence of Brazil, China, India, Indonesia and Russia (hereafter referred to as the Big Five) as major players in the world economic, political and environmental scene; rapid technological advances, particularly in information and communications technologies; and the unprecedented increase in world-wide trade and investment.

... an historic coincidence of interests for OECD and non-OECD economies.

Today's globalising world economy thus provides an historic coincidence of interests for OECD and non-OECD countries. Closer linkages between these economies are beneficial for sustained economic growth, improving living standards, eliminating poverty and promoting environmental sustainability, which will strengthen the foundations for global political stability. There is now a window of opportunity for improving welfare, and moving along an accelerated path toward sustainable development, in all areas of the world, by shifting economies onto a higher performance growth path.

A number of major challenges must however be tackled:

A number of challenges have to be tackled...

– Further progress will be necessary in the liberalisation of trade, investment and financial flows, and in strengthening the rules-based multilateral system, to facilitate a deepening of economic integration between the world's economies.

– In some OECD countries, there are already signs of a backlash against globalisation, which is sometimes blamed for persistent unemployment, widening income inequality and de-industrialisation. To tackle these problems, a wide range of domestic policy reforms is necessary and are being undertaken to make their economies and societies more adaptable and dynamic, so as to realise more fully the benefits of intensifying linkages with a growing number of non-OECD economies, while enhancing social cohesion.

– Although they have benefited from globalisation, some dynamic and emerging economies are concerned about the short-term adjustment costs of further opening up their markets – to both imports from industrial countries, and imports from lower cost developing countries.

– In most other non-OECD economies, far-reaching policy changes are needed, particularly in those countries where the transition from a developing to a more advanced economic structure has in many cases (notably Sub-Saharan Africa) just begun.

– Globalisation can promote a more efficient and less environmentally-damaging pattern of economic development, but these gains may be overwhelmed by the pollution and resource use associated with the increased scale of economic activity.

... but the world economy is not in uncharted waters.

And yet, the world economy is not in uncharted waters. The market-based economic system, with its wealth-creating energy, had already revealed a capacity to operate on a global basis by the later years of the 19th Century, when transport and telecommunications technologies first made it possible to move goods, capital, information and people around the world on a significant scale. A "New Global Age" is now taking shape, where all countries can be active players, where people currently trapped in poverty can aspire to much better levels of material well-being. That inspiration has become a working agenda for the international community, including both OECD and non-OECD countries, which are attempting to realise their coincidence of interests.

The international community is adopting longer term goals...

In this regard, the international community has been increasingly adopting longer-term policy goals, notably in respect of free trade and investment, into the next century. APEC has adopted the goal of free trade and investment in the Asia-Pacific region by 2020. The 34 democracies of the western hemisphere agreed to devise a Free Trade Area of the Americas (FTAA) by 2005, building on the North American Free Trade Agreement. The European Union has also agreed with 12 Mediterranean countries (Euromed) to establish free trade by 2010. In addition, the OECD Development Assistance Committee has selected goals for economic well-being, social development, and environmental sustainability and regeneration in developing countries (mostly for the year 2015).

... while this report presents a vision for the world in 2020.

This report presents two alternative visions of the world economy in 2020: a slow-track reform and adjustment scenario (a "business-as-usual" scenario) and a high performance vision of the world economy, where governments seize the challenge of realising a "New Global Age". This high performance vision is not a forecast, instead it seeks to paint a plausible scenario for the world economy, if governments undertake a wide range of necessary policy reforms. In this context, this report sets out some of the key economic, social and environmental policy challenges for realising a "New Global Age", along with some implications for the role of international organisations, including the OECD, in helping to achieve this goal.

II. GLOBALISATION AND STRUCTURAL CHANGE

OECD economies have undergone great structural changes...

Structural change has been a pervasive trend in all economies (see Section 1.1 of the Analytical Report). In OECD economies, the agricultural sector has declined steadily through the twentieth century. Industrial employment rose as a share of the total in most OECD countries until about 25 years ago, when its share began to fall, while employment in services has been rising in all OECD countries (see Table 1.1). Knowledge-intensive industries and firms have had above-average employment growth, but there has been a decline in the demand for low-skilled workers relative to skilled labour.

... partly due to the growth in international trade.

In the post-war period, progressive liberalisation of international trade among the OECD countries has been an important factor contributing to the growth of OECD living standards, as well as structural change in OECD economies. Sharp cuts in tariffs and non-tariff barriers, together with continued falls in transportation and communication costs, stimulated international trade, more than reversing the decline in the ratio of trade to GDP that had occurred in the inter-war period (Figure 1.1). International financial movements have also been liberalised among OECD economies. Although the dismantling of financial barriers began later than in the case of goods trade, it has been more complete and there are now no significant barriers to financial flows in almost all OECD countries.

The impact of non-OECD economies is growing...

Non-OECD economies did not have a major influence on OECD economic performance during the 1950s and 1960s. But from the 1970s, Hong Kong, Korea, Singapore and Chinese Taipei (the so-called NIEs) expanded their manufactured exports rapidly, when most other non-OECD economies were still wedded to import substitution and heavily dependent on primary commodity exports. The past decade has seen the adoption of free market principles by a wide range of countries, which has spurred their economic growth and integration into the global economy:

... particularly for the Big Five.

– The former centrally-planned economies (including **Russia**) have now made great progress in moving toward a market system.

– **China** has emerged as the world's fastest growing economy, and the share of its population in poverty has halved since its historic policy shift in 1978.

– **Indonesia** has successfully transformed itself from a heavily resource-dependent economy in the early 1980s to a major exporter of light manufactures, and also seen a large drop in poverty.

– **India**'s reforms began in earnest in only 1991, but the effects on growth and exports have already been visible.

– **Brazil** and many other Latin American countries have made dramatic progress in stabilising, reforming and restructuring their economies, with positive results, following the lost decade of the 1980s.

– **Sub-Saharan Africa** has been slower to emerge from the crisis of the 1980s, with GDP growth in the 1990s being lower than the previous decade. Nevertheless, growth performance and prospects are now improving, with an increasing number of countries moving to strengthen macroeconomic management and to liberalise their economies.

In many respects the Big Five are major players. They are the only non-OECD countries to have both populations in excess of 100 million and GDP above $100 billion. They also play an important role across many fields, such as trade, investment, agriculture, energy (including nuclear) and the global environment. Along with other countries, they each play a leadership role in their respective regions and in international relations.

Non-OECD economies are becoming a driving force in globalisation...

There has been an acceleration of globalisation over the last decade, with non-OECD economies being a driving force, through their linkages with OECD economies, and amongst themselves (see Tables 1.2 and 1.3). However, the pace of integration of non-OECD economies into the global economy has been very uneven. While the aggregate ratio of non-OECD countries' trade to GDP has increased during the past ten years, ten countries from East Asia and Latin America accounted for more than 70 per cent of this increase. Africa has been largely bypassed by the surge in private capital flows and is still overwhelmingly dependent on ODA.

... which is beneficial to both OECD and non-OECD economies.

Economic integration among economies of different levels of development (like OECD and non-OECD economies) can be even more beneficial than among economies at the same level of development. Dynamic non-OECD economies, which have been able to grow more than twice as fast as OECD countries, represent an increasingly important market for OECD exports. OECD FDI in developing economies can be more profitable than home investment, and is often associated with exports of capital and intermediate goods to establish the investment. And portfolio investment in emerging markets can be a source of higher risk-adjusted returns and portfolio diversification. Further, consumers in OECD countries can make substantial gains, as the price of goods imported from developing countries is typically much lower. Resources in OECD countries are then be freed for higher productive uses, such as skill-intensive services and capital equipment, some of which is exported to non-OECD countries, stimulating in turn their development.

... but involves adjustment costs.

Such economic integration does involve adjustment costs, especially for low-skill workers and industries. This can lead to tensions, especially when they coincide with high and persistent unemployment in many OECD countries, which can manifest themselves in social strains and protectionist pressures. In order to minimise these tensions and facilitate these structural changes, governments must ensure flexible labour and product markets, foster the upgrading of skills and competencies, and reform social policies in ways that support the adjustment, rather than hinder it, so as to maximise the benefits of closer linkages with non-OECD economies.

III. THE WORLD IN 2020

The world economy in 2020 will be marked by...

The world economy in 2020 will clearly be vastly different from that of today, in the same way that the world of today is greatly changed from 1970. Trends in population and technological change will clearly mark the future (see Sections 2.1, 2.2 and 2.3).

... a large increase in the non-OECD population;

Demographic prospects are more predictable than many other parameters over the period to the year 2020 and will be very different between most of the OECD countries and most of the area now outside the OECD. In very broad terms, one key economic implication is that the non-OECD area will continue to have a comparative advantage in the export of labour-intensive goods and services, even if the more advanced non-OECD economies become more service-oriented.

... ageing populations in OECD countries;

Population growth in the non-OECD area, especially in Africa and parts of South Asia, will account for virtually all the increase in the world population, from 5 billion in 1990 to about 8 billion in 2020. Africa, China and India could each have a population of around 1.3-1.4 billion. Experience has shown that rapid population growth often threatens the sustainability of development. It has also demonstrated that both general development progress (especially when it empowers women) and targeted reproductive health and family planning efforts, can make a major impact in enabling countries to reach more sustainable population balances. Meanwhile, population ageing will take place in most OECD countries (particularly in Japan where the population will decline) reflecting the end of the baby boom, falling fertility rates and increased lifespans. In many non-OECD countries, notably China and Russia, populations will also age over the period to 2020.

... and technological change.

The interrelated factors of deeper integration among the world's economies, improvements in human capital and technological change will provide the potential for continued growth in world prosperity. Information technology, biotechnology, advanced materials, alternative energy sources and improved transport could play major roles. For example, advances in microelectronics will accelerate world-wide communications, providing the foundation for the transformation of existing social and economic relationships into a "global information society". This may lead to the adoption of more flexible and innovative strategies and forms of work organisation, both at the domestic an global levels.

Realising the benefits of these trends...

Fully realising the potential benefits of these developments over the next 25 years will depend in large part on government policies. If governments makeonly slow progress in liberalisation of international trade and finance, fiscal consolidation, policies enhancing, innovative capacity and technology diffusion, or further reforms to product and labour markets, OECD countries might see a similar productivity performance to that of the past 25 years, which was much lower than earlier decades after World War II. In these circumstances, annual economic growth could fall to around 2 per cent, compared with almost 3 per cent over the last 25 years. Poverty and marginalisation may remain a major problem for a large number of non-OECD economies, unless they develop the necessary

14

... depends on government policies. domestic capacity for development, in terms of policy frameworks, governance systems, and social, human and physical capital. Much worse scenarios could be envisaged – for example, a reversal of the process of globalisation could lead down the road of global fragmentation, with adverse effects for prosperity and political stability.

Projections of prosperity... If, however, OECD and non-OECD governments move towards global free trade and capital movements, and undertake the above reforms, world prosperity could be very much greater (the "New Global Age" scenario) (see Figures 2.1 to 2.4). In these circumstances, some of the broad lines of the world economy could be:

... for OECD economies; – Real GDP per capita in the OECD area would be 80 per cent higher in 2020 than in 1995 (compared with about 50 per cent higher under business as usual).

– Progress would be far more dramatic in the non-OECD world, given its generally lower level of development. Real GDP per capita would be around 270 per cent above 1995 levels by 2020 (compared with about 100 per cent under business as usual).

... and even more so, for non-OECD economies; – Non-OECD economies would continue their catch-up towards the development levels of OECD countries, as average GDP per capita could rise from only 15 per cent of that in the OECD area to some 30 per cent in 2020 in purchasing power parity terms (PPP) (all GDP figures are in PPP terms, unless otherwise specified).

... to which there would be a big shift in global economic weight. – Higher growth in the non-OECD area would also mean a big shift in global economic weight, as the non-OECD share of world GDP would rise to 67 per cent in 2020, from 44 per cent in 1995 (see Figure 2.5). The Big Five could together account for more than one-third of world GDP in 2020, about the same as the OECD countries, partly due to their very large populations. In PPP terms, China could be the world's largest economy, equivalent in size to half of the OECD. However, in market price terms, China would be the world's third largest economy, after the United States and Japan, with its GDP representing 7 per cent of the world's total in 2020.

– The non-OECD area could become a driving force in the global economy, and OECD economic performance could depend more and more on their policies and performance, particularly the Big Five. The non-OECD share of world trade could increase significantly, from one-third at present to one-half in 2020 (lower than its share in PPP-based world GDP, as trade takes place at market prices).

The strong boost in prosperity would improve capacities to deal with many problems... A "New Global Age" would provide a strong boost to standards of living the world over, with low-income families in particular seeing great reductions in poverty, increases in life expectancy and substantial progress in primary education, gender equality, basic health care and family planning. This prosperity would improve the foundations for global stability. It would also improve the capacity to deal effectively with a great host of problems, such as:

... environmental; – the unsustainable use of water, fisheries and forests and other natural resources as well as a growing range of environmental problems at local, national, regional and global levels;

... urban; – the likely substantial urbanisation in many non-OECD countries, as their economic structure moves toward industry and services. According to the United Nations' estimates, the urban population of less-developed countries may rise from one-third in 1990 to over 50 per cent by 2020, with a dramatic rise of a large number of megacities, particularly in Asia;

... and social.   — the challenges for social policy, especially for OECD countries with ageing populations, in a world of greater competitive pressures and structural change, partly arising from closer linkages with non-OECD countries.

IV. REALISING THE VISION FOR 2020

Realising the vision...   The trends of globalisation, and the prospects for a "New Global Age", hinge on the ability of individuals and groups of human beings to adapt to, and ultimately to steer, unprecedented pressures and opportunities for change. Within all countries, and among countries, profoundly new and complex challenges of governance are emerging, with the need to find new balances between the roles of the state and other public and private actors. Changes in governance will be needed to help populations to form realisable expectations for both their economic security and their own responsibilities, if social cohesion and political stability are to be secured.

... poses challenges for governance;

... and requires macroeconomic stability.   Stable and sustainable macroeconomic policy will be a precondition for taking full advantage of the opportunities provided by globalisation, as well as for successful structural reform. This is particularly true for non-OECD countries with a history of macroeconomic instability. Low inflation rates and sustainable fiscal positions reduce the riskiness and improve the allocation of saving and investment, thereby stimulating economic development. They also allow economies to take advantage of the opportunities offered by global financial markets. Experience has shown, such as in the recent episode in East Asia, as well as in earlier similar episodes, that capital inflows can be destabilising and suddenly reversed if investors fear a deterioration in macroeconomic conditions. The impacts of such capital movements on the real economy can be severe when the domestic financial system, especially the banking system, is fragile.

a.   Strengthening the multilateral system

Trade and investment

The multilateral system must be strengthened.   A fundamental requirement will be maintaining, and indeed strengthening wherever possible, a free and open, rules-based multilateral system for the benefit of all participants (see Sections 1.2 and 1.3). Creation of the World Trade Organisation (WTO), whose membership is becoming progressively universal, has provided the legal basis for the new multilateral trading system as a single, indivisible undertaking and established clear authority to negotiate and manage a comprehensive set of rules for international trade in both goods and services. Both China and Russia, as major players outside the WTO, are defining their policies and programmes with a view to gaining membership of the WTO. Uruguay Round commitments involve further very substantial reduction of border barriers. And post-Uruguay Round agreements have already been achieved in the areas of basic telecommunication services and information technology, with negotiations still scheduled in several other areas.

OECD countries are negotiating an MAI.   In the area of international investment, OECD Member countries are negotiating a multilateral agreement on investment (MAI), which seeks to establish a broad and legally-binding multilateral framework based on high standards for the liberalisation of investment regimes, with strong investor protection and effective dispute settlement procedures. The MAI will be a free-standing international treaty open to all OECD Members and the European Communities, and also to accession by non-OECD countries – a number of which have indeed indicated their wish to accede.

But both border and domestic barriers need to be tackled...   While the present base for the multilateral system is promising, policymaking remains confronted with many challenges. Some difficult border barriers remain in OECD countries in areas such as agriculture, while the barriers to trade and capital movements are generally higher in non-OECD countries. And the attention of the multilateral system is now increasingly focused on behind-the-border barriers, as the multilateral system is not yet equipped with all the necessary institutional instruments for promoting greater market openness and competition in a globalising environment.

... in the competition-oriented agenda.

Pursuing a competition-oriented agenda implies: *i*) incorporating investment protection and liberalisation disciplines on investment in the WTO; *ii*) considering options for addressing private anti-competitive behaviour within the multilateral trading system; and *iii*) ensuring that countries' regulatory reform efforts go hand-in-hand with efforts to enhance market access opportunities. In the latter context, a notable challenge is to develop greater incentives to promote mutual recognition agreements or conformity standards for goods and services.

Protectionist pressures will continue to be a threat.

As in the past, protectionist pressures will continue to be a threat. These may be accentuated by growing competition as service sectors become increasingly internationalised, and electronic commerce and cheaper transportation quicken the linkages between economies. And accommodation of a larger presence of non-OECD economies in the world economy will require substantial adjustments (see Section 2.8), such that continued trade frictions will be a virtually unavoidable part of the globalisation process – not only between OECD and non-OECD economies, but also among non-OECD economies. As a greater number of developing countries continue integrating into the global economy, protectionist voices in OECD and advanced non-OECD economies may question the "fairness" of developing country trade, through concerns about core labour standards, and claims that countries with less stringent environmental policies are "eco-dumping". Governments will need to be extremely vigilant that legitimate concerns about core labour standards and the environment are dealt with through appropriate policies and not used as a means for backtracking from the liberalisation path, and that unjustified concerns in this area, advanced as an excuse for protectionism, are firmly resisted.

Internation migration

OECD countries will remain desirable destinations for migration...

Liberalised trade and capital flows bring the prospect of increased living standards for the global economy. Whilst higher growth for poorer countries is commonly held to reduce the incentive to migrate, there are stages and situations where the reverse is the case. For example, increased living standards could increase the awareness of the possibilities of migration and also the means to incur the costs of migration. Hence, precise predictions about the effects of globalisation on the incentives to migrate are difficult to make. However, despite this and other social and political uncertainties, it seems likely that the majority of OECD countries will remain desirable destination countries for migration well into the next century.

Beyond the traditional economic and social benefits and costs that play a part in migration policy, if governments deem it opportune, immigration could also help mitigate some problems which are likely to arise from the projected ageing of OECD populations and labour forces over the coming decades. First immigration could, in principle, act as a brake on demographic ageing, thereby helping to alleviate possible sectoral labour market imbalances. Second, realistically absorbable increases in immigration could help support at least a small share of the growing fiscal burden associated with ageing populations through higher output and increased tax revenue.

... which could help mitigate some problems due to ageing populations.

Future negotiations which aim to achieve the liberalisation of trade and capital flows may well have to deal with barriers to international migration of labour too. It seems likely that access to overseas labour markets will be an item under negotiations concerning access to their domestic markets for goods, services and direct investment.

Financial markets

*Closer **OECD**/non-**OECD** financial linkages are in prospect...*

The desire for broad portfolio diversification will drive close financial linkages between OECD and non-OECD economies (see Sections 1.3 and 2.5). Scarcity of capital in emerging economies and the effects of ageing populations in many OECD countries will also contribute to global financial integration, fostering world-wide growth through a more efficient allocation of capital. But the process will also need to be supported by appropriate policies in both OECD and non-OECD countries.

*... but **OECD** countries should reassess remaining capital restrictions;*

In the OECD area, restrictions on capital movements have been almost entirely eliminated, except for regulatory constraints on the capacity of certain investors to invest abroad. These regulations need to be reassessed in order to provide scope for greater portfolio diversification, including in emerging markets, which would enable institutional investors to improve risk-adjusted returns on their assets.

*... while non-**OECD** countries have a more challenging policy agenda;*

In most non-OECD countries, the policy agenda is much more challenging. Though the speed and sequencing of liberalisation will have to be determined by each country in light of its particular circumstances, policies should be geared to the ultimate objective of full integration into the global financial system. To this end, countries will need to set in place forward-looking programmes for the removal of capital controls, the liberalisation of cross-border financial services and the abolition of restrictions to market access by foreign investors and institutions.

... and financial structures and frameworks must be modernised.

The process of financial integration will also require stepped up efforts on the part of all countries to modernise their financial structure and to upgrade their regulatory/supervisory frameworks. Effective implementation of a comprehensive programme of financial regulatory reform will be particularly important for those countries whose financial systems are least developed and whose regulatory systems do not conform to international standards; progress in this area will be key to enable them to engage in, and reap the benefits from, liberalisation.

Taxation

International considerations are becoming more important for national tax policies.

With the dismantling of other obstacles to the free flow of capital, financing and investment decisions will become even more sensitive to tax differentials (see Section 3.1). More generally, while all countries need to ensure a favourable business climate, countries will face challenges in maintaining their domestic tax bases in the face of the globalisation of economic activity. As a result, international considerations will become more important in the determination of national tax policies, increasing the potential for conflicts between tax administrations of different countries as well as between tax administrations and tax payers.

... increasing the need for international rules of the game.

Under these circumstances, it is more urgent than ever to develop international rules of the game upon which the whole world tax community can rely, in order to reduce potential tensions between countries and to minimise tax barriers which would facilitate a better international allocation of resources. Against this background, the OECD is developing global principles and rules in the fields of tax treaties and transfer pricing and for counteracting international tax evasion and avoidance, and an increasing number of non-OECD countries are associating themselves with these rules.

However, new challenges are already emerging. Among them, tax havens or large overseas tax preferences and the implications of the evergrowing importance of multinational companies and cross-border transactions through global communication technologies, in particular the use of the Internet, stand out for their potential importance in terms of their impact on tax policy and administration in home countries. At present, these fields of taxation are characterised

18

by an absence of internationally-agreed standards and rules, with an attendant risk of substantial revenue losses and difficulties in effective tax enforcement for all countries. A co-operative approach will be needed to limit the scope of tax evasion and to adjust tax rules to cope with the development of electronic commerce, the increased integration of financial markets and new payment methods.

b. Labour market and social policies in OECD countries

OECD *labour markets*

A new global age requires greater flexibility...

A "New Global Age" holds in prospect a world of much greater prosperity, but also a world of greater competitive pressures and more rapid structural change, where greater labour (and product) market flexibility will be necessary (see Section 3.1). While OECD governments have made considerable progress in structural reform of financial markets and international trade, there has been less progress in reforms of labour and product markets. Poor labour market performance has been a growing source of concern for OECD countries in the past three decades with high and persistent unemployment in many countries, and rising income inequalities in other countries.

... to achieve smooth structural adjustment and maintain social cohesion.

In the "New Global Age" scenario, it has been assumed that OECD governments introduce and sustain the policy reforms of the OECD Jobs Strategy which would achieve a substantial improvement in labour market performance (especially in Europe where unemployment rates could fall to around 5 per cent, reversing the rise that started in the early 1970's). In the period to 2020, OECD labour markets will continue to be challenged by the related objectives of achieving smooth structural adjustments and maintaining social cohesion. While there could be very much higher standards of living for all, there may also be forces working to widen income distributions, as labour market pressures from trade and technology favour skilled labour relative to unskilled and semi-skilled labour. Ageing populations will also shrink labour forces, increase dependency ratios and put upward pressure on health costs, particularly in Japan and to a lesser extent Europe. All these tensions may threaten social cohesion, requiring a broad policy response.

Social policy

Social policy must enhance the capacity to change...

Change is often resisted because of the risk of being a loser rather than a winner (see Section 3.1). Furthermore, too large a gap between rich and poor may leave some groups being unable to exploit effectively the opportunities to improve their position which in theory exist. Social and lifelong learning policies which enhance the capacity of individuals to adapt to structural change will be doubly beneficial, ensuring both that new opportunities are fully exploited and also limiting resistance to change. By offering a degree of security, social protection can encourage individuals to take risks and be flexible in responding to changes in their economic circumstances.

... social security will need to be re-designed;

OECD institutions for social security will need to be re-designed for an era when many employees are likely to change jobs, and possibly even careers, several times during their working life. Restructuring of national labour markets could include a continuing decline in relative demand for unskilled labour. Social and educational policy must focus on these unskilled workers. They are at risk of long-term dependency and social exclusion.

... long-term social exclusion must be avoided;

The long-term exclusion of individuals and families from society because of lack of labour market opportunities is unacceptable, both socially and economically. Income support systems should not confine themselves to the provision of an adequate existence for those excluded from work; they need to emphasise reinsertion in the labour market, rather than just provide an adequate existence for those excluded from work. Lifelong learning will be essential for ensuring that workers remain productive, especially as populations and labour forces age over the coming decades. Failure to respond to social distress risks reinforcing an intergenerational cycle of welfare dependency and social exclusion. With pressures on public finances leaving little prospect for new net public expenditure being made available to meet these risks, resources will have to be found by withdrawing from lower-priority areas of spending.

... "active ageing" is a key-policy.

The emphasis will need to be on "active ageing", encouraging individuals to participate fully in society regardless of their age. Social protection systems should be adapted to facilitate a more flexible transition from work to retirement. This would contribute to a reversal of the current trend towards ever earlier retirement, which would in itself be the single most effective step that OECD countries could take to reduce the pressure on their social protection budgets. At the same time, raising the effective age of retirement will require major changes in the attitudes of workers, employers and society. But it is necessary and desirable and, with increased flexibility in employment parities, does not imply more of a lifetime spent in work.

c. Consolidating integration of non-OECD countries into global economy

Integration into the global economy...

The dynamic and emerging economies from East Asia and Latin America, and those "transition economies" which have made great progress in their economic transformation, are demonstrating that integration into the global economy is a powerful strategy for accelerating growth and development (see Section 3.2). At the same time, a large number of developing economies, particularly in Africa, have seen their participation in trade and FDI fall.

... is a powerful strategy for development;

Looking toward 2020, one of the central challenges will be facilitating and consolidating the further integration of non-OECD economies into the global economy. Freeing trade and investment globally would of itself help the integration of non-OECD countries into the global economy, by improving the "coherence" between OECD countries' trade and investment policies, and their development co-operation efforts. More fundamentally, however, active participation in the global economy depends upon the strengthening or creation of effective economic, human, social and institutional capacities. Most non-OECD countries need institutional reforms necessary to promote "supply-side" capacities, notably private sector development and enterprise competitiveness.

... and is a key-challenge.

It requires improved "supply-side" capacities...

Privatisation, the legal framework for enterprises, regulatory reform and taxation and competition policy are all important areas for reform efforts. In conjunction with strong macroeconomic policies and financial management, reforms in these areas will lay the basis for internationally-competitive domestic enterprises and help attract FDI, thus building up the linkages with the global economy. For poorer developing economies, ODA can play a catalytic role in helping countries build their domestic capacities, including the capacity to integrate into the global economy, by increasing exports, attracting private capital and becoming less dependent on aid.

... for poorer countries ODA can play a catalytic role.

The development co-operation effort, which is a complex and difficult undertaking involving many bilateral and multilateral agencies, is now being more clearly focused on the 1996 Statement of the OECD Development Assistance Committee (DAC), "Shaping the 21st Century: the Contribution of Development Co-operation". This statement sets out the progress that could be achieved by 2015 in terms of economic well-being, social and political development, and environmental sustainability. The achievement of the goals of the strategy hinges on effective self-help, supported by better co-ordinated development co-operation, which should raise the level of domestic resource mobilisation and the productivity of all resources through improved governance and greater reliance on a private-sector based economy.

d. Policies for sustainable development

The global environment

Closer **OECD/non-OECD**
linkages can promote
sustainable development...

Closer linkages with non-OECD economies can promote a more efficient and less-environmentally damaging pattern of economic development: by shifting economic production from raw-materials based manufacturing to knowledge-based service industries; through the development and diffusion of cleaner technologies; by alleviating poverty and the associated environmental effects in non-OECD economies; and by generating additional wealth to finance environmental improvement (see Sections 1.4, 2.4 and 3.4). In these ways, there could be a decoupling of economic growth from pollution generation and resource consumption, which would promote sustainable development.

... but increasing economic activity and
population can intensify
demands on the environment;

However, countervailing forces could offset these positive trends. Overall resource consumption and pollution might well increase despite lower levels per unit of output, due to increasing economic activity and population. In addition, even if the environmental and welfare effects of linkage-intensive development were positive globally, the distribution of environmental pressures would vary according to comparative advantages in assimilative capacity and resource endowments. Indeed, the material and resource intensity of OECD countries may decrease at the same time as the demands on the environment in non-OECD economies increase. Questions have already been raised about the equity and sustainability of such trends.

... non-OECD economies will account
for a growing share
of environmental problems.

The projected shift in economic weight from OECD countries to the non-OECD economies, as well as continued population growth, suggest that the non-OECD economies – and the Big Five in particular – will account for a growing share of regional and global environmental problems (see Table 1.10). Over the next few decades, pressures will be intensified not only globally but also regionally, nationally and locally; for example, through growing consumption of fossil fuels and associated emissions, rising volumes of hazardous and other wastes, the concentration of populations in "mega-cities", more intensive agriculture, timber and fisheries exploitation, and growing demands for fresh water resources. There are already indications that these pressures could intensify insecurity and conflict within and between countries.

For economic development
to become sustainable...

If economic development in the period to 2020 is to become sustainable, it is essential that effective environmental policies be implemented nationally and internationally. The 1992 United Nations Conference on Environment and Development (UNCED) in Rio helped to raise awareness and promote new initiatives, but in June 1997, at the United Nations General Assembly Special Session, the Programme for Further Implementation of Agenda 21 stressed the deep concern of governments that the overall trends for sustainable development are worse today than they were in 1992. The implementation of Agenda 21 is, the document concluded, more urgent now than ever. Greater political will and vision will be required to ensure that the global economy develops in a sustainable manner.

... requires effective environmental
policies, both nationally and
internationally;

Prioritisation of local environmental problems based on analysis of costs and benefits, and consultation among stakeholders will provide a firm basis for cost-effective use of financial and other resources as well as promote local "ownership" of solutions. The application of market-based instruments, wherever possible, and the enactment and enforcement of realistic environmental standards complement this approach. Equally, international rules of the game will be needed to address common problems. However the realisation of these mutual interests is impeded by more intense competition among countries, the unequal distribution of costs and benefits which result from major policy initiatives, and different attitudes and priorities among countries concerning global and other environmental problems. It is of fundamental importance to develop effective mechanisms to implement the principle of "common but differentiated responsibilities" elaborated at UNCED.

... and more effective integration of environmental considerations in international relations.

Policies for environmental protection and globalisation can and should be designed to be mutually supportive and complementary. Improved information about environmental impacts and greater consumer demand for green products are likely to make it more profitable for private firms to develop environment-friendly technologies and business operations. Without progress in this area, there may be additional opposition to policies promoting globalisation, as well as demands to use trade and investment instruments as substitutes for inadequate environmental policies. This underlines the need for environmental considerations to be more effectively integrated into the evolving system of international economic relations.

Energy

Energy consumption will grow substantially, particularly in the Big Five...

The high-performing scenario for the world economy will be accompanied by substantial growth in fossil fuel consumption, mostly by non-OECD economies, particularly the Big Five (see Sections 2.4, 3.3 and 3.4). As many non-OPEC oil fields are expected to pass their periods of peak production over the period to 2020, world oil supply is likely to become ever more concentrated on Middle East producers. On the basis of past experience, concentration of oil supplies in one region can be a source of market volatility.

... and green-house gas emissions could double between 1992 and 2020...

Closely linked to fossil fuel use is the global environmental issue of greenhouse gas emissions and the associated threat of global warming. The accelerated growth of output over the next 25 years in the high-performance world is expected to increase substantially atmospheric emissions of CO_2 (see Figure 2.14), which could double between 1992 and 2020. Since the non-OECD area is expected to grow particularly rapidly, an important share of the increase in emissions will be concentrated there.

...without international agreements to reduce emissions.

However, these projections do not take into account the aim of limiting the future growth of greenhouse gas emissions at 1990 levels, as agreed by Annex I Parties under the United Nations Framework Convention on Climate Change. OECD Member countries and other Annex I Parties are expected to agree on legally binding targets for emission reduction at the Kyoto Conference in December 1997. A key issue in the design of a new agreement is provision for the use of market mechanisms to improve the cost-effectiveness of emission reduction strategies. Joint implementation and international greenhouse gas emission trading could provide a means to benefit from differences in marginal cost of reduction across countries.

The challenge will be to contain and reduce greenhouse gas emissions in energy production and from sectors such as transport and industry , which to a large extent involves reducing dependence on fossil fuels without significantly reducing living standards. Establishing realistic and binding emission reduction targets is a first step forward to stimulate the market for technology innovation and change. In addition to strategies to enhance international co-operation through the use of joint implementation and emission trading, a host of other policies will be required at the domestic level to achieve long-term emission reduction. As in the case of other pollutants, governments should ensure that the private sector faces prices for fossil fuel use that fully reflect the social costs, including those associated with possible global warming. Eliminating subsidies on fossil fuels would be an important step forward.

Nuclear energy has much less impact on global warming, but safety and waste disposal issues must be resolved...

It is, of course, unclear which among the currently available alternative energy sources might in the long run displace fossil fuels, or whether technologies not yet discovered will prove to be the answer. One alternative is nuclear power, which is now in wide use in many OECD and non-OECD economies and accounts for about 17 per cent of the world's electricity generation. However, concerns about safety and waste disposal have sharply increased political resistance in many countries in the past 25 years. If these issues can be resolved, the way would be paved for increased use of a resource that has much less impact on global warming than fossil fuels. However, doing so will require a broad policy approach embracing technical, economic and political considerations.

... to facilitate increased use of nuclear energy.

Agriculture

World food demand will increase substantially...

Population growth, rapid urbanisation, income increases and dietary changes are likely to increase food demand substantially in the period to 2020 (see Sections 2.4 and 3.3). 80 per cent of the increased demand could originate from the non-OECD region, with half of that coming from China and India alone. This will put pressures on agricultural production as most of the increases in production will have to come from yield increases. While there is great scope for increasing yields, important policy reforms will be necessary to meet the necessity of producing enough food for the world's population in 2020, such as: providing a stable market-oriented framework; expanding national and international research focused on developing countries; assuring agricultural sustainability and sound management of resources; and reducing food marketing costs in low-income developing countries. Improving agricultural productivity in Sub-Saharan Africa will, however, be a major challenge. Despite some encouraging results in a few countries, there are no clear signs yet that agriculture in Africa is playing the key role in the economy that is needed if the continent is to develop in a sustainable way.

... but policy reforms in major producers would improve productivity.

Rapid income growth will remain the single most important factor driving long-term food demand in China. Long-term projections, however, show that China will neither "starve the world" nor return to being a large net exporter of grains. Instead it will become a more significant importer of grains and, as income growth continues, a growing importer of higher value food products, although China also has the potential to export specific high value food products. India's success in agriculture owes a lot to high rates of public investment in irrigation, research and, most importantly, input subsidies. The long-term outlook suggests that India's agriculture will be able to meet domestic food demand. It will also be able to accommodate a relative switch from food grains to higher value food products and defend its position as a small net-exporter of agricultural commodities. Russia's food imports by contrast are expected to increase. Rising overall imports will be characterised by a further shift from bulk commodities to consumer-ready food products. However, over the long term, Russia and Ukraine have the potential to develop production, in particular of cereals, provided the necessary economic and technical prerequisites are fulfilled.

V. FOSTERING A COMMON COMMITMENT TO A HIGH-PERFORMING WORLD

Globalisation will require greater international co-operation...

In the rapidly changing and globalising world economy, there will be an even greater need for international co-operation so as to realise a "New Global Age". There is a growing internationalisation of many policy issues, which were previously more domestic in nature. And countries are increasingly confronted with a common set of policy problems, on which common solutions through identification of best practices and multilateral surveillance can be effective. In this context, the whole range of international institutions – from the United Nations system and the World Trade Organisation, to the International Monetary Fund and the multilateral development banks, and to the many regional groupings – is now working to develop policies that promote economic prosperity, political security (including through enhanced economic interdependence) and sustainable development.

Strong political leadership, particularly in OECD countries, will be necessary to convince public opinion of the need to strengthen engagement in the international system. Such leadership will also be necessary to strengthen popular support for policy reform and dealing with adjustment problems. Governments must implement a focused and credible communication strategy to raise public understanding of the stakes involved.

The OECD can make an important contribution to global change and reform through its role as a catalyst and pathfinder in international economic co-operation, at the disposal of its Members and, through them, the international community. It is an inter-governmental economic organisation, global (though not universal) in its membership, with unique structures and methods of work relying on dialogue and peer pressure to bring international co-operation and collaboration to policies which carry international implications. Along with other international organisations, it can make a contribution towards the realisation of a "New Global Age" through its analysis of important national and international problems, in a multidisciplinary and forward-looking way, which can help underpin sustainable development. This includes designing policies to balance carefully the triangular paradigm of economic growth, social stability and effective governance.

New emerging issues have always been a priority of the OECD. In recent years, major studies have been undertaken on employment/unemployment, ageing populations and regulatory reform. Also the OECD is strengthening its function of setting up binding and non-binding rules-of-the-game as exemplified in the work on the MAI, bribery and taxation. In this regard, the OECD can play, in the coming years, a special role in preparing new issues (such as electronic commerce, cryptography and governance), especially those not ready for international negotiations, and forging co-operative bargains and shared norms.

The OECD itself is destined to be greatly shaped by the process of globalisation in the period ahead. Already, the OECD has accepted five new Members since 1994, and expanded its co-operation with non-OECD countries, reflecting its global approach to policy analysis and dialogue. The OECD will no doubt have new Members, as further countries share the membership's common economic and democratic principles, and the respect for human rights. As their weight in the global economy increases, co-operation with non-OECD economies will become an increasingly important aspect of OECD's role of addressing the most pressing socio-economic problems and opportunities challenging Member countries.

The plurality of international institutions requires a clear focus in each institution on its unique contribution and a greater awareness of building complementarities and synergies with other institutions. In this regard, OECD works closely with other international organisations, with a view to exploiting synergies and minimising duplication. Such co-operation will need to continue, particularly with organisations in the Asia-Pacific region, whose economic weight will increase markedly in the period to 2020.

The global economy will involve a widening range of actors. Globalisation is mainly driven by the private sector through its global strategies. And pressure groups, many of which now operate on an international basis, are important players in many global issues, such as the environment. OECD's policy dialogue activities should provide greater scope for dialogue between all relevant players, so as to strengthen broad-based consensus-building.

To strengthen the foundations for global governance, more effective partnerships will be necessary between OECD and non-OECD countries, particularly in light of the latter's prospective important weight in the global political, economic and environmental scene. In this context, the OECD should give consideration to strengthening further the special partnerships t with the Big Five. Some will probably become OECD Members in the period to 2020. In the meantime, involving these economies more in OECD's multilateral surveillance could be mutually beneficial. These economies can have important impacts on OECD countries (and *vice versa*), especially in areas like the environment, trade and investment flows, and food and energy security.

... for OECD to bring together the major players of the world economy.

Through its close co-operation with the Big Five and other important non-members, the OECD brings together the major players in the world economy in a non-negotiating forum. In this way, the OECD can also be an important global link between many other processes of international co-operation, which are either more restricted or regional, such as the G7, APEC and ASEM. It also provides a forum for policy dialogue on contentious issues which lie at the heart of sustainable development, such as subsidy and tax reform, consumption and production patterns, and trade and investment policies. This can help lay the basis for more productive outcomes from other fora, such as major United Nations conferences, World Trade Organisation and APEC Ministerial meetings.

ANALYTICAL REPORT

CHAPTER 1.   GLOBALISATION AND LINKAGES

The world has undergone impressive political and economic transformations in the past quarter century. The widely used term "globalisation" describes the forces that have produced rapid growth in world trade (at twice the rate of world output), even faster expansion of international capital flows, the integration of the world's financial markets, and the apparent acceleration in global diffusion of new technologies. Important policy and institutional changes, notably declining barriers to trade, the creation of a multilateral trade regime and the dismantling of capital controls, have been a driving force behind globalisation. Remarkable changes in technology which have sharply reduced costs of transport and communications have also promoted greater trade, financial integration, and transfer of technology. While global integration was in a sense quite advanced in the late 19th and early 20th centuries, the "new global age" is different in several respects: i) the ratio of trade to world GDP is now well above its pre-Depression peak (see Figure 1.1); ii) the scale of capital flows has reached unprecedented levels; iii) communication, information and transport technologies are contributing to a major restructuring/decentralisation of production structures; iv) multinational corporations have achieved a truly global presence, and the number of countries

◆ Figure 1.1. **World exports**
(as a per cent of GDP)

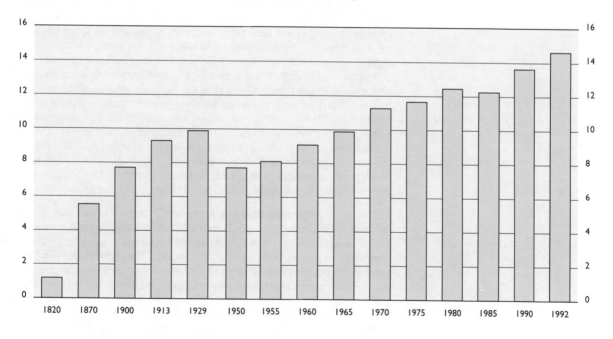

Note: GDP is expressed in 1990 dollars at PPPs.
Source: A. Maddison, Monitoring the World Economy, 1820-1992,
   OECD Development Centre Study.

Table 1.1. **Share of services in G7 countries**
Per cent

	1970	1980	1994
1. In total civilian employment			
Canada	60.7	65.6	72.9
France	45.9	53.9	65.8
Germany	42.1	50.0	58.4
Italy	39.2	46.6	60.1
Japan	46.9	54.2	60.2
UK	51.3	58.9	69.9
USA	59.5	64.9	72.3
2. In GDP (at constant prices)			
Canada	61.9	63.7	65.7 [a]
France	53.5	57.0	61.6 [a]
Germany	46.6	51.8	61.6 [a]
Italy	50.5	51.6	53.6
Japan	54.4	60.2	63.1 [a]
UK[c]	55.3	59.0	72.0
USA	59.8	65.3	69.3 [b]

a) 1995.
b) 1993.
c) Based on current prices.
Sources: *Labour Force Statistics*, OECD (section 1); OECD (1996), *Services: Statistics on Value Added and Employment* (section 2).

with home-grown multinationals has increased significantly; *v*) the current phase of globalisation does not involve permanent shifts of labour between countries (though there is a great deal more temporary movement of skilled labour); and, most importantly *vi*) globalisation now involves many more – and an increasing number of – countries (most of which did not exist as independent nation-states during the earlier globalisation era). While the decades following World War II were characterised principally by closer integration among OECD countries, in the past two decades new players have entered the stage. A rapidly expanding group of developing countries and economies-in-transition have taken deliberate – and in many cases drastic – steps to open their economies wider to the outside world. They are liberalising imports, promoting exports, encouraging foreign investment, and decontrolling foreign exchange regimes. Such linkage-intensive development strategies have already propelled a number of non-OECD countries into the front ranks of trading nations and recipients of foreign investments.

These developments have greatly altered the landscape. No longer principally raw material suppliers, non-OECD countries have emerged as major trading partners in a range of manufactured goods, and OECD manufactured imports from those countries now exceed primary commodity imports. Through the 1960s and 1970s, a handful of relatively small developing countries, mostly in East Asia, pursued successful development strategies based to a significant degree on the export of manufactures. They have now been joined by many other countries, including some very large ones – *e.g.*, China and lately India – whose integration into the world economy will have a significant impact. Another large potential for reaping mutual trade benefits exists in countries which, up to now, have been left behind in the world-wide integration process. Indeed, trade/GDP ratios have risen markedly only in non-OECD countries in East Asia and Latin America, while they have dramatically fallen in Sub-Saharan Africa and, though less so, in the Middle East and the North African region. Africa has been largely by-passed by the surge in private capital flows and is still overwhelmingly dependent on official development aid.

The increasing emergence of powerful, low-cost competitors in international markets of manufactures has reinforced the long-term trend in advanced industrialised OECD countries towards services and within industry towards high- and medium-tech products. These trends have been more pronounced in the sectoral composition of employment than of output (see Table 1.1). The declining weight of employment in industry, sometimes referred to as "de-industrialisation", is a normal consequence of much higher productivity growth in manufacturing than services and a higher average demand-income elasticity for services than for manufactures.

The compositional changes in sectoral output and employment, experienced by all OECD countries, have been accompanied by rising demand for skilled labour and declining demand for unskilled labour. This phenomenon is attributable, in part at least, to the expanding trade with low-income countries as this opens up new export markets for skill-intensive products and services, while at the same time squeezing out non-competitive low-skill industries and firms. The employment consequences of this pressure have not, however, been evenly felt among OECD countries. They have been more pronounced where skill- and sectoral wage dispersion has failed to respond to changes in relative labour scarcity and/or where labour market policies have not succeeded in redirecting labour from declining to expanding sectors of the economy. In this context it is relevant to note, however, that the present size of imports of manufactures from newly industrialised low-wage countries is still too small to explain much of the fallen demand for low-skill workers.

1.1. Evolving Trade and Investment Links between Countries and Regions

As noted in the first OECD *Linkages* study (1995), trade and investment links between the OECD countries and non-OECD countries have grown considerably over the past 25 years. The globalisation trends noted in that study have further accelerated since the early 1990s (see Figure 1.2). There is an increasingly close connection between the emerging patterns of world trade and of global investment, as the internationalisation of production stimulates trade flows between investors' home and host countries and as cross-investments between countries proliferate. While intra-OECD trade still accounts for almost three-fourths of world trade and intra-OECD foreign investment for roughly two-thirds of total OECD outward foreign direct investment (FDI), these shares are declining and should continue to drop as barriers to trade and investment fall in non-OECD countries. Trade and investment links have also grown dramatically among non-OECD countries over the past decade.

Trade links

The establishment of the General Agreement on Tariffs and Trade (GATT) following World War II was an important factor in the resumption of rapid trade growth after the protectionist policies of the inter-war period. Successive rounds of trade negotiations have culminated in the successful completion of the Uruguay Round in December 1993. Since then, world trade has recorded its fastest-ever growth rates. World trade growth doubled from 4 per cent per annum between 1980 and 1993 to 8 per cent 1994-96, outpacing world output growth by a widening margin. For OECD countries, trade has grown very rapidly in recent years, with non-OECD countries figuring prominently in that growth. From 1990 to 1993, intra-OECD trade grew at half the rate of world trade growth, while OECD trade with non-members grew much

◆ Figure 1.2. **Globalisation trends: trade and investment flows**
(1970 = 100)

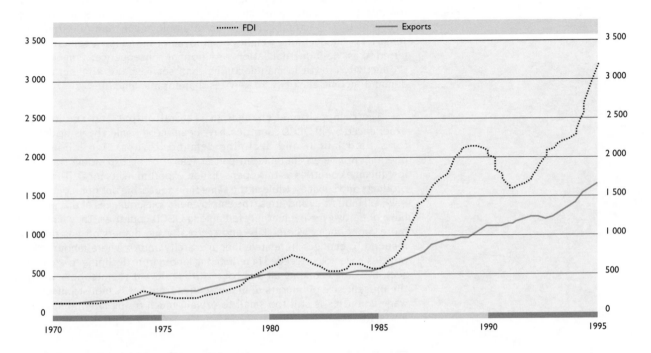

Source: WTO and UNCTAD Websites.

Table 1.2. **World trade growth, 1990-95**
Annual percentage change

	1990-93	1994-95
World trade	4.4	9.2
OECD intra-trade	2.2	7.8
OECD-NMEs trade	7.5	10.7
NME intra-trade	8.8	15.2

Note: At constant prices.
Source: Based on OECD and WTO data.

faster (see Table 1.2). In 1994-95, intra-OECD trade staged a strong recovery, remaining, however, well below the 10.7 per cent growth in OECD trade with non-members.

Of OECD regions, Japan has by far the largest proportion of its trade outside the OECD area, amounting to half of its total trade in 1995 (see Table 1.3). For the United States, the non-OECD share was one-third and for the EU one-fifth (37 per cent when intra-EU trade is excluded). OECD trade growth during the 1990s has been particularly rapid with the central and eastern European economies (though from a rather small base) and with the five large emerging economies, the "Big Five": Brazil, China (including Hong Kong), India, Indonesia and Russia. For the OECD as a whole, the Big Five represent about one-fourth of trade with non-OECD countries and 6.6 per cent of all trade – well below the 10 per cent share of the Dynamic Asian Economies (DAEs). For the US and Japan, the share of the DAEs is twice that of the Big Five.

32

Table 1.3. **OECD trade with non-OECD economies**
Percentages

	Trade structure, 1995[a]			Trade growth 1990-95[b]		
	Japan	EU-15	USA	Japan	EU-15	USA
All NMEs	52	19	35	11.8	11.7	11.9
Big Five	13	5	8	15.0	12.7	16.2
DAEs	28	4	16	14.7	12.3	11.3
CEECs	1	3	1	2.5	19.1	3.3

a) Total value of exports plus imports divided by total trade.
b) Growth rates refer to current $ values.
Source: Based on OECD and WTO data.

◆ Figure 1.3. **Trade with the Big Five, 1985-1995**
(total trade, $ billion)

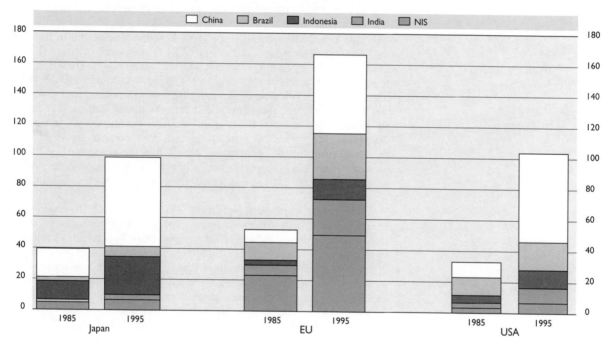

Source: OECD NEXT Data Base.

China stands out among the Big Five as the major OECD trading partner and the one with whom trade has grown fastest. For example, US trade with China increased seven-fold between 1985 and 1995 while US trade with the other Four doubled. For the US and Japan, bilateral trade with China in 1995 was larger than that with the other Four combined. The European Union is the largest OECD trading partner of the Big Five, with a total trade volume of $170 billion in 1995 compared to $100 billion for the US and for Japan (see Figure 1.3). Its trade structure with the Big Five is also much more geographically balanced, including significant trade flows with the Newly Independent States of the former Soviet Union (NIS), Brazil and India.

Intra-trade of non-OECD countries (NME) has also grown impressively in the 1990s. In 1990-93, it grew at twice the rate of world trade and since 1994 its growth rate has almost doubled to over 15 per cent per annum.

Table 1.4. **Intra-non-OECD trade, 1995**
As percentage of total trade

	LA	CEECs	Africa	ME	Dev. Asia	Share of non-OECD in the region's trade
Latin America	**20.3**	1.1	1.1	1.2	6.1	29.8 (28.3)
CEECs	1.7	**19.1**	1.2	1.6	8.7	32.3 (49.9)
Africa	2.3	1.7	**9.6**	2.8	10.1	26.6 (19.1)
Middle East	2.0	1.8	2.3	**8.4**	20.1	34.6 (31.2)
Developing Asia	1.7	1.6	1.3	3.6	**34.9**	43.1 (36.9)
Share of the region in total non-OECD trade	4.7 (4.3)	3.4 (7.2)	2.0 (2.1)	3.4 (4.0)	24.4 (16.9)	37.9 (34.5)

Note: In parenthesis, 1990 figures.
Source: Based on WTO data.

Though intra-NME trade still represents only 11 per cent of world trade, its share in total NME trade has steadily risen to 38 per cent in 1995 (Table 1.4). The intra-NME trade share is uneven across regions: rather low in Africa, although rapidly increasing since 1990; high but decreasing in the Central and Eastern European Countries (CEECs), because of the collapse of Comecon in 1991; slowly increasing in Latin America – partly reflecting new regional trade agreements – and in the Middle East; and rapidly rising to high levels in developing Asia, where intra-NME trade accounts for 43 per cent of the region's total trade and intra-regional trade for 35 per cent. Developing Asia is by far the largest beneficiary of intra-NME trade growth. On average, two-thirds of intra-NME trade now involves developing Asian countries (up from 49 per cent in 1990). While the share of the CEECs has declined markedly, the successful switch towards EU countries and more generally, towards hard currency countries explains much of this change.

The product composition of OECD's trade with non-OECD economies has changed dramatically in the past decade. For non-OECD economies as a whole, the share of primary products in total exports to OECD countries fell by half, to 29 per cent, in the decade to 1995. This steep decline and the parallel rise of manufactured goods has been associated with a marked shift in terms-of-trade against primaries, the declining primary resource intensity of OECD output and the emergence of new competitive suppliers of manufactures. Between 1985 and 1995, international trade in manufactures has grown at an annual rate of 6.5 per cent, far above the 2.5 per cent registered for primary products. Developing countries and regions that have re-oriented their exports towards manufactured goods have strongly benefited from favourable international demand, while those that have remained dependent on primary commodities have suffered. The DAEs, whose share of manufactured goods in total exports is the highest among non-member country groupings – 87 per cent in 1985 and 95 per cent in 1995 – also reported the largest increase in total exports over the ten-year period.

For the Big Five, primary goods fell as a share of their total exports to the OECD from almost two-thirds in 1985 to less than one-fourth in 1994, with manufactured exports rising correspondingly. The shifts were large in Indonesia, Russia and especially China, where the share of primary goods dropped from 48 per cent to only 8 per cent. Japan's and the EU's imports from the Big Five remain much more heavily weighted towards primary goods (33 and 32 per cent of total 1994 imports respectively) than those of the United States, where the share of manufactures in imports from the Big Five rose from 55 per cent in 1984 to 93 per cent in 1994.

◆ Figure 1.4. **OECD industrial trade with non-OECD economies, 1994**
($ billion)

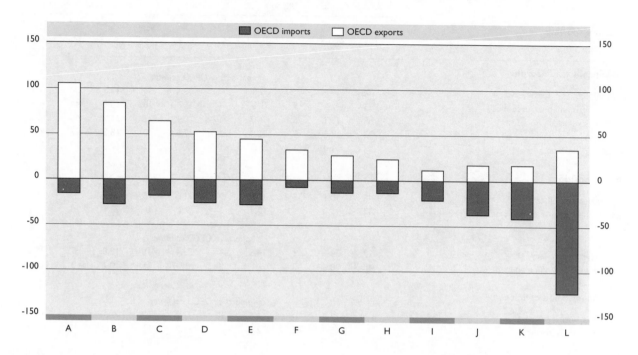

Note: A: Non-electrical machinery. B: Chemicals and pharmaceuticals. C: Motor vehicles. D: Iron, steel and metal products. E: Electrical machinery, F: Aerospace. G: Scientific equipment. H: Telecommunication equipment. I: Rubber and plastic products. J: Computer and office equipment, K: Other manufacturing. L: Textile, wearing apparel and leather.
Source: OECD NEXT Data Base.

While the OECD countries have a thriving two-way trade with non-OECD economies in manufactured goods, net OECD exports remain strongly positive in non-electrical machinery, chemicals and pharmaceuticals, motor vehicles, iron and steel, electrical machinery and aerospace (see Figure 1.4). On the basis of R&D intensity, the OECD classifies all these sectors as medium-tech or high-tech. Conversely, OECD countries are strong net importers of low-tech goods. This pattern is broadly consistent with intuitions about comparative advantage, although net exports of medium-tech goods are higher than of some high-tech goods, which merits comment. The industry groupings are highly aggregated and disguise some important intra-industry variation in the technology-intensity of specific products or production processes. For certain high-tech goods (notably telecommunications equipment and computers, and their respective components), production is highly internationalised and a very significant share of trade between the OECD and the non-OECD economies consists of intra-firm trade between OECD-based multinationals and their foreign subsidiaries, with the latter performing relatively labour-intensive assembly operations. Also, the non-OECD countries are an increasingly heterogenous group of countries, with some having quite advanced technological capabilities. For instance, a number of East Asian countries are competitive producers of electronics goods in their own right, with Korea and Chinese Taipei manufacturing and exporting large quantities of personal computers and peripherals, consumer electronics equipment, and semiconductors and other components.

Table 1.5 gives a more detailed picture of OECD trade with major non-member economy groups. The product classifications shown include those where OECD countries are significant net exporters, those in which OECD

Table 1.5. **OECD trade with selected non-OECD groupings, 1985-1994**

Trading partners **Sectors showing**	All non-OECD		Big Four		China		DAEs		Other non-OECD	
	$bn 1994	% 85-94	$bn 1994	% 85-94	$bn 1994	% 85-94	$bn 1994	% 85-94	$bn 1994	% 85-94
Significant trade surplus	*Exports from OECD countries*									
Non-electrical machinery	108	10.6	12	9.6	11	12.4	34	19.9	50	6.6
Chemicals and pharmaceuticals	85	8.7	9	1.5	4	2.2	28	15.8	44	8.0
Motors vehicles	65	13.1	5	16.7	4	10.1	17	24.9	40	10.3
Aerospace	33	14.0	3	20.0	3	17.5	10	18.5	17	9.6
Scientific Instruments	27	11.4	2	7.6	1	2.1	12	17.6	12	8.9
Mixed position	*Exports from OECD countries*									
Electrical machinery	45	10.1	3	8.9	2	11.0	16	14.7	24	7.8
Computer and office equipment	33	13.0	1	12.1	1	9.9	8	20.1	23	11.3
	Imports to OECD countries									
Electrical machinery	27	23.1	1	14.8	4	83.4	10	18.8	12	22.8
Computer and office equipment	40	28.6	0	4.4	2	109.4	35	30.2	3	15.0
Significant trade deficit	*Imports to OECD countries*									
Textiles, wearing apparel	124	13.8	16	16.5	32	27.9	37	6.2	39	16.0
Other manufacturing	36	15.4	4	12.3	7	51.3	11	11.8	13	13.2

Note: Big Four comprises Brazil, India, Indonesia and NIS. First column: value of trade, 1994 ($billion), second column: annual growth rate, 1985-94 (%).
Source: OECD NEXT Data Base.

exports to and imports from non-OECD economies are both large, and those where OECD countries are significant net importers. Annual trade growth rates from 1985 to 1994 show the consistent importance of the DAEs as markets for OECD exports. Moreover, the growth in their imports from the OECD has been particularly strong for capital goods (non-electrical and electrical machinery, computers and office equipment) and motor vehicles. China stands out for its rapid emergence as a major supplier to OECD markets of labour-intensive products (notably textiles and clothing but also other manufactures), while it plus the Four (Brazil, India, Indonesia and Russia) offer increasingly important markets for a range of OECD exports. Indeed, the capacity of these countries to export manufactured products to OECD countries depends crucially on their imports of capital and intermediate goods from OECD countries. For non-electrical machinery, motor vehicles and aerospace, the Big Five already represent large markets for OECD exports. With the notable exception of China, in particular *vis-à-vis* the United States, OECD countries do not report any large merchandise trade deficits with non-OECD economies.

The bulk of world merchandise exports originate from large-scale enterprises and trade within globally diversified multinationals accounts for an increasing share of that trade. Although small and medium scale enterprises (SMEs) are not usually associated with globalisation, it is estimated that they account for about a quarter of OECD direct manufactured exports and play an even larger role in indirect exports via supplier networks. Among the large OECD economies, the export share of SMEs varies from 13.5 per cent in the case of Japan to 70 per cent in the case of Italy and their export contribution appears to have been rising in recent years. Advances in

	Table 1.6. **Merchandise and service trade, 1995** As a percentage of output	
	Merchandise	Services
OECD	27.6	4.7
US	28.2	3.5
Japan	19.3	3.4
EU-15	27.2	5.9

Note: Intra-EU trade is excluded.
Source: Based on the Global Trade Analysis Programme (GTAP) Data Base.

communications and other technologies and in the organisation of production have enabled more SMEs to compete internationally.

Trade in services

Trade in commercial services grew at double the annual rate of merchandise trade between 1980 and 1995 (8.7 per cent versus 4.5 per cent). In 1995 it amounted to roughly $1 trillion, or 23 per cent of total world trade of merchandise goods and services. Despite this strong growth, trade intensities for commercial services remain far below those for merchandise (see Table 1.6). Trade in services is considerably underestimated by current balance-of-payments statistics which fail to reflect transactions like cross-border intra-firm exchange of technical and financial advice, remote data processing and transmission, and the revenue from services offered in the host country by foreign affiliates of multinationals.

The OECD countries and a few Asian non-OECD countries dominate world services trade, with the European Union accounting for about 45 per cent of services exports, Asia (including Japan) just over one-fifth and North America just under one-fifth. The United States is by far the largest single exporter of commercial services: in 1994, those exports reached $185 billion, roughly two-thirds of which went to other OECD countries. Apart from travel and transportation, business, professional and technical services represent the largest category of US exports to non-OECD countries, followed by education.

With further reductions in communications and travel costs deriving from technological innovation and deregulation, and the ongoing liberalisation of services trade in the aftermath of the Uruguay Round (witness the recent agreement on trade in telecommunications services), commercial services trade should continue to grow briskly. Also, with faster GDP growth in non-OECD economies, the growth of their demand for services will likely outpace that of OECD countries. In 1994, the average share of services in the Big Five's total GDP was 44 per cent, ten percentage points higher than in 1980, and that share should continue to rise for some time as their economies become more mature. Closer integration into the global economy should itself generate demand for more reliable and sophisticated services. For example, efficient producer services – including global communications and air freight transport – help exporters respond quickly to overseas customers' needs and changing market trends; efficient financial services are needed to conduct international commerce, manage cash reserves, and hedge foreign exchange risks. Those OECD countries with highly developed service industries should enjoy a rather strong comparative advantage in supplying these emerging services markets.

Technological innovation – particularly in communications and information processing – is expanding significantly the scope for services tradeability. The blossoming of global computer networks and the falling costs of global communications will provide new opportunities and incentives for the unbundling and international outsourcing of information-intensive service activities – *e.g.*, research and development, computer programming and software development, back-office administrative tasks, marketing, customer service, inventory management, legal services and even, to some degree, education and health care. For instance, the Memorial University of Newfoundland, Canada, has held a series of teleconferences on such topics as immune response, hepatitis, and emergency paediatrics for physicians in Kenya and Uganda. Distance learning via the Internet is another activity still in a very early stage of development. While OECD countries may have a comparative advantage in supplying some remote services, developing countries could emerge as sizeable exporters in a number of areas – and in some they already have, as with India's software industry and with data entry, computer programming and insurance claim processing in several Caribbean countries and the Philippines.

How large is the potential for developing countries to serve as remote service providers to the OECD countries? One recent study lists three criteria for such long-distance services: they must *i*) be information-intensive (and by implication relatively labour-intensive), *ii*) require limited direct contact with customers, and *iii*) not involve manipulation of physical objects. On these criteria, perhaps 12 to 16 per cent of service jobs in the G7 countries could be substituted by long-distance provision. These figures indicate only technical feasibility, but OECD firms' decisions on whether or not to outsource particular services depend also on relative costs and strategic business objectives. Recent evidence suggests that, in general, long-distance service provision becomes an attractive option for large companies only when cost savings are on the order of 30-40 per cent. On the assumption that firms would actually find outsourcing economically attractive for only 10 per cent of those jobs for which it is technically feasible, as of 1990 the potential additional market for long-distance service exports from developing countries to the G7 was estimated at around $40 billion (or 6 per cent of non-OECD countries' total exports).

Investment links

Increased capital mobility is one of the principal phenomena associated with globalisation. Reductions in transport and communications costs, capital account opening, financial market deregulation and privatisation of state enterprises have combined to create a conducive environment for growing cross-border financial flows. On the supply side, the globalisation of production has stimulated FDI. Pension funds and other institutional investors in OECD countries have sought greater portfolio diversification through investment in overseas markets, including emerging markets. On the demand side, low international interest rates and improved creditworthiness have spurred new international bond issues as well as an upturn in international bank borrowing. From 1990 to 1995, borrowing on international capital markets rose by one-fourth, to $1.3 trillion, and the share of non-OECD economies in total international borrowing rose to almost 10 per cent (from 7.7 per cent in 1990). The share of non-OECD economies is already highly significant in net total international bank lending –20.4 per cent – and in total FDI flows –35.2 per cent.

While figures on gross cross-border financial flows are useful in assessing international capital mobility, figures on net capital inflows indicate how much non-OECD economies rely on foreign capital to balance their savings and investment needs. Total net capital flows to non-OECD economies amounted to $330 billion in 1996, two and a half times their 1990 level (see Figure 1.5). While there was some adverse reaction in capital markets to the 1994 Mexican financial crisis, it appears to have been short-lived and geographically concentrated. While the Mexican shock was transmitted directly to most Latin American stock and

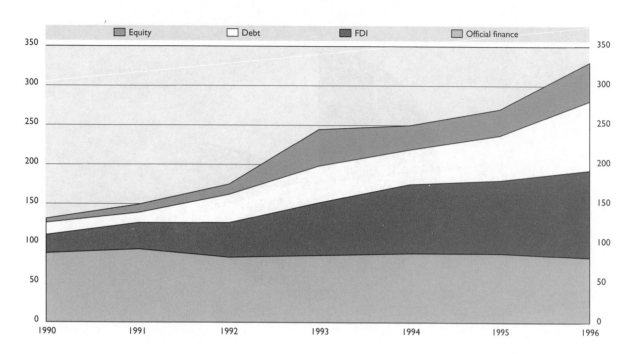

◆ Figure 1.5. **Net resource flows to non-OECD economies**
($ billion)

| | Equity | | Debt | | FDI | | Official finance |

Source: OECD and World Bank.

debt markets, it seems to have been felt only mildly in Asian securities markets. Moreover, price falls were related to fundamental measures, as countries with weaker external positions suffered higher negative spill-over effects and more open countries appear to have suffered less contagion. This finding may signalreversal or default is higher. (It should also be borne in mind that the evidence on contagion effects has been established in the presence of important official financial assistance to Mexico and Argentina.) In 1994-1995, net capital flows to non-OECD countries continued to rise, though at a slower rate than from 1990 to 1993, while figures for 1996 indicate renewed strong growth.

The trend towards a more prominent role for private flows and the relative decline of official development finance has accelerated in recent years. The share of private flows in the total has risen from one-third in 1990 to almost three-fourths in 1996. Direct private financing – as opposed to bank intermediated financing – now accounts for almost 60 per cent of total net flows to non-OECD economies. FDI represents more than half of private financing for non-OECD economies, and debt financing increasingly relies on bonds. Since 1994, FDI-related net capital inflows to non-OECD economies have been larger than official development finance. In spite of a significant decrease in 1994-1995, portfolio equity investments recovered in 1996 to break their 1993 record high and now amount to 14 per cent of total net capital inflows to non-OECD economies.

Between 1990 and 1995, total net capital inflows to the Big Five have increased by 150 per cent, and the share of the Big Five in total capital flows to non-OECD economies has increased from 26 per cent to 34 per cent (see Figure 1.6). China has been, by far, the largest recipient outside the OECD area, with net capital inflows increasing fivefold since 1990. The acceleration has been quite widespread, however, with the other Big Five countries, as well as other developing areas – including Sub-Saharan Africa and South Asia – all reporting larger capital inflows over this period. From 1990 to 1995, Indonesia, Brazil, Russia and India were

◆ Figure 1.6. ***Destination for international capital, 1995***
(per cent of total net resource flows to non-OECD economies)

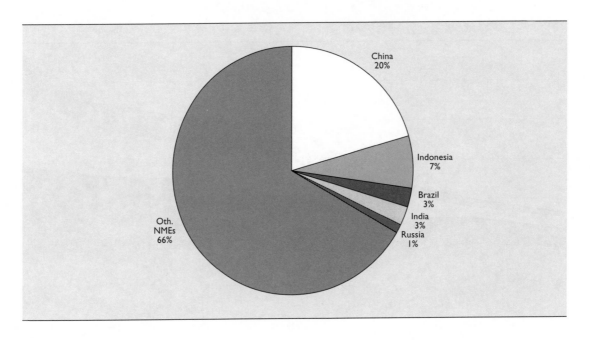

China
20%

Indonesia
7%

Brazil
3%

India
3%

Russia
1%

Oth.
NMEs
66%

Source: OECD and World Bank, World Debt Tables.

respectively the second, fourth, fifth and seventh largest recipients of net foreign capital flows amongst developing countries (excluding Mexico and Korea). India's share, however, has steadily declined since 1985. As for Russia, the huge net resource inflow ($38.4 billion) that took place during 1990-1993 was short-lived and since 1994 it has slowed to a trickle ($2 billion a year). Thus far, Russia has benefited least among the Big Five from growing international private capital flows, though it has the potential to attract much larger flows, particularly into its fossil fuels and other resource sectors.

The composition of capital inflows varies significantly across developing regions. Latin America continues to be considerably more debt-dependent than East and Southeast Asia, with a heavy recent reliance on short-term debt instruments. (Some Southeast Asian economies have also significantly increased their short-term debt exposure to finance widening current account deficits and, in Thailand, the recent steep fall in the value of the baht has significantly raised borrowers' foreign currency obligations.) A closer look at the patterns of foreign capital flows to the five largest emerging economies confirms the increasing role of private financing over the 1992-1995 period (see Figure 1.7). Low-income countries that have been able to attract private capital over the past decade – like China, India and Indonesia – have significantly reduced their reliance on official development finance (grants, public multilateral and bilateral loans). For China, official development finance accounted for slightly over 10 per cent of total net capital inflows. Moreover, China has a rather "healthy" composition of private capital inflows since it relies largely on FDI. Elsewhere, net private capital flows have been more heavily weighted towards private loans and more volatile equity portfolio investments.

Africa, meanwhile, remains overwhelmingly dependent on official development assistance (ODA), which has fallen in real terms by roughly 15 per cent since 1990. The bulk of private capital is still heavily concentrated in a small number of countries (see Figure 1.8) and has largely bypassed Africa. No

◆ Figure 1.7. **Composition of net resource inflows, 1992-1995**

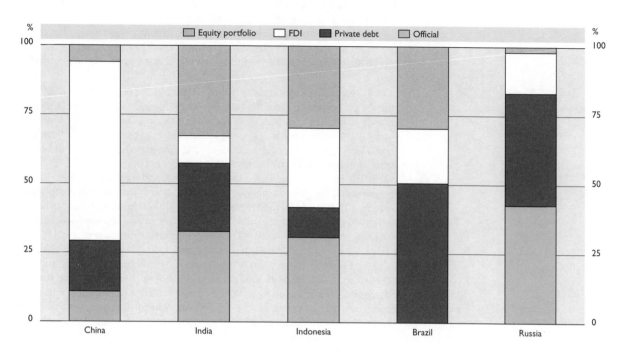

Source: OECD and World Bank, World Debt Tables.

◆ Figure 1.8. **Distribution of capital flows to non-OECD economies, 1994**

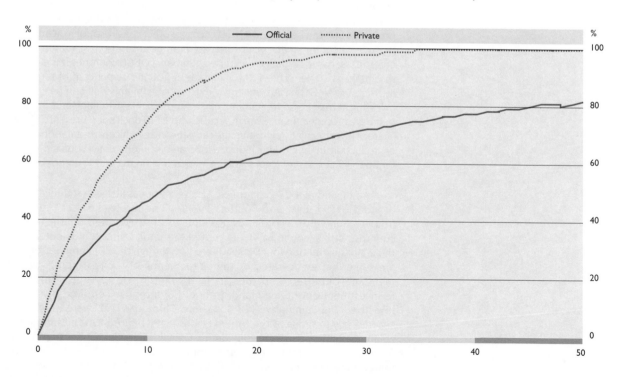

Note: Largest fifty recipients of net private and official flows.
Source: OECD Financial Flows Data Base and World Bank.

Sub-Saharan African country figures among the largest 20 recipients of private capital, which collectively accounted for well over 90 per cent of total private flows in 1994. (South Africa does rank among the top 30 countries in terms of the cumulative stock of inward foreign investment.) The Figure also indicates the much stronger concentration of private flows than of official flows, with the top 20 recipients of ODA accounting for only about 70 per cent of the total.

Foreign direct investment is by far the largest net private financial flow to non-OECD countries. Over the past decade, FDI outflows from OECD economies rose at 15 per cent per year – i.e., more than twice as fast as their nominal GDP. Intra-OECD flows grew at the same rate as flows to non-OECD economies. Two forces have driven this sharp increase: the development of global strategies to access foreign markets by an increasing number of companies in OECD countries (including small and medium size companies), and widespread liberalisation of international investment regimes around the world. The sectoral composition of outward FDI flows from the G7 countries has shifted quite significantly since the early 1980s, with primary sector FDI falling steeply and tertiary sector (services) FDI rising steeply. In the case of the USA, outbound primary sector FDI more than halved to 13 per cent between 1982-84 and 1991-93, while tertiary sector FDI increased from 29 per cent to 50 per cent. For Japan, over the same period, the primary share fell from 21 to 6 per cent and the tertiary share rose from 46 to 66 per cent. (This includes all FDI and not just that destined for non-OECD economies.) The service sector differs somewhat from manufacturing in that the response to liberalisation is more likely to be through increased foreign direct investment than through increased trade since many services remain non-tradeable.

Within industry, foreign investment is most evident in high-tech and medium-tech sectors (e.g., computers and other electronics, pharmaceuticals and other chemicals, and automobiles) because these sectors have the most pronounced firm-specific advantages (e.g., proprietary technical and managerial know-how). In the case of electronics, automobiles, and other assembly-type industries, there is also scope for the decomposition of production into discrete processes that can be located wherever cost or other considerations dictate. While the overwhelming share of FDI activity is undertaken by large multinational enterprises, based on data for a limited number of OECD countries it is estimated that perhaps 10 per cent of SMEs engage in FDI and 10 per cent of total FDI is attributable to SMEs. An unknown but probably significant number of SMEs investing abroad do so to maintain close supplier links with large multinationals that have preceded them. Even in sectors where FDI does not represent a sizeable share of investment, foreign sourcing can generate significant internationalisation of production. In the clothing industry, for example, international sourcing accounts for up to 40 per cent of total sourcing, depending on the OECD home country.

Among non-OECD economies, Asian economies attract a significant share of FDI. In 1995, East and Southeast Asia alone received 62 per cent of FDI flows to non-OECD economies. Excluding China, East and Southeast Asian countries still account for 40 per cent of the total. China stands out as by far the major destination for FDI (see Table 1.7), though the FDI numbers for China are somewhat exaggerated by the phenomenon of round-tripping, whereby mainland Chinese companies transfer funds to Hong Kong affiliates for re-investment on the mainland, with all the incentives enjoyed by "foreign" investors. The cumulative FDI flows into China, 1991-95, were $114 billion, second only to those to the United States ($198 billion). Given China's much smaller economy and even considering China's higher investment ratio, these flows represent a much larger share of China's gross fixed capital formation (an average 11.6 per cent, 1990-94, compared to 4.1 per cent for the United States). Among developing economies, Brazil and Indonesia are also major destinations for FDI, in particular for OECD FDI. For developing countries as a

Table 1.7. **Host countries for FDI, 1991-1995**
Cumulative flows, $ billion

1 [a]	United States	198.5
2	**China**	**114.3**
3	United Kingdom	86.3
4	France	63.1
5	Spain	43.5
8	Mexico	32.0
11	Malaysia	24.3
12	Singapore	23.1
14	Argentina	18.0
18	**Brazil**	**12.4**
19	**Indonesia**	**11.9**
45	**India**	**2.9**
46	**Russia**	**2.6** [b]

a) Ranking.
b) 1994-1995 only.
Source: OECD Foreign Direct Investment Data Base; IMF (1996).

group, the contribution of FDI to gross fixed capital formation has increased from an average of 2.8 per cent (1984-89) to 5.2 per cent (1990-94).

In 1995, while 65 per cent of all FDI to developing countries went to Asia, about 27 per cent went to Latin America. Brazil, Argentina and Chile attracted an estimated $4.9 billion, $3.9 billion and $3.0 billion, respectively. Despite increases in absolute dollar terms, levels of FDI flows into both South Asia remain quite modest, at $2.7 billion. Over the past couple of years, annual FDI flows to Africa have been around $5 billion. Nigeria accounts for around 60 per cent of the overall total FDI to Sub-Saharan Africa, while Egypt alone accounts for almost one-half of all FDI into North Africa. Although FDI to the 48 least developed countries rose 29 per cent in 1995, it amounted to only $1.1 billion out of total flows to developing countries of $100 billion.

Privatisation, especially of infrastructure, has played an important role in attracting FDI to Latin America and more recently Central and Eastern Europe. From 1988 through 1995, FDI inflows accounted for more than half of infrastructure privatisation revenues in developing economies (two-thirds for privatisations involving telecommunications companies). Because in many developing countries the scope for privatisation is far from exhausted, more FDI of this type is likely to occur. More generally, the increase in the scope for strategic alliances with local companies has reflected the development of a large, diversified and outward-looking business sector in non-OECD economies. Joint ventures and mergers and acquisitions have also become a common form of FDI, gaining importance relative to more traditional forms such as green field investments and extension of existing plants.

Whereas until recently OECD countries were the overwhelmingly dominant source of FDI, during the 1990s that has begun to change. From 1990 to 1994, the developing country share of global FDI outflows rose from 7 to 17 per cent. By far the major source of non-member country FDI are the Dynamic Asian Economies together with China. In 1995, FDI outflows from developing Asia amounted to $43 billion, representing 90 per cent of all developing country outflows. In Latin America, Brazil and Chile have also begun generating relatively large FDI flows.

1.2. Trade and Competition Policies

Both OECD countries and non-OECD economies can reap potentially large benefits from closer integration. Since the early 1990s, OECD trade with non-members has grown much faster than intra-OECD trade. While this owes something to depressed economic conditions in several OECD countries, trade with non-members will likely continue to grow as a share of OECD trade in a longer time horizon. There are several potential benefits from closer trade links. First, consumers enjoy real income gains as they are able to import goods that would cost more to produce domestically. Domestic producers also benefit from the sourcing of materials and components from lower cost overseas suppliers. Second, imports act to intensify competition, keeping domestic inflationary pressure at bay and stimulating cost-reducing process innovation and demand-enhancing product innovation. Third, growing export markets can provide opportunities to exploit scale economies, particularly where domestic markets are small. Fourth, for OECD countries, further trade liberalisation will tend to favour skill-intensive industries and services, creating relatively high-paid jobs for those with the appropriate skills. As observed in the DAEs, imports of capital equipment and high-quality intermediate goods from OECD countries are crucial to the success of their own export industries. Also, OECD engineering industries have benefited enormously from expansion of the infrastructure that has supported growth in non-OECD economies, and their infrastructure investment demands are slated to rise steeply in coming years. Fourth, as non-OECD countries' services sectors are liberalised, attractive new opportunities should arise for competitive OECD service providers (*e.g.*, media and information services, software, education, financial services, insurance, real estate, management consulting, and others). To give some indication of the potential, in 1994 US exports of services to non-Japan Asia and Latin America amounted to approximately $60 billion, which was almost as large as its service exports to Europe.

Completion of the Tokyo and Uruguay Rounds (UR) of trade negotiations has resulted in broad-based tariff reductions and the easing of some of the important non-tariff barriers, greatly enhancing the prospects for reaping global welfare gains from further trade expansion. Efforts to calculate the benefits of the UR suggest prospective gains of anywhere from one per cent up to about a five per cent increase in world GDP. While the five per cent estimate derives from a study that includes a broader range of effects than some others, all the studies probably underestimate the hard-to-measure dynamic benefits of trade. The measured gains come from low tariffs on industrial goods, tarification of many quantitative restrictions, and the abolition of the Multi-Fibre Arrangement. One of the most significant non-quantifiable benefits of the Round for non-OECD economies is the greater credibility of their own trade policy regimes as a result of their tariff bindings, as well as their acceptance of the obligations on non-tariff measures. Moreover, through this single undertaking, the NME signatories of the UR have committed themselves to the rules of the game on market access in industrial and agricultural goods, intellectual property rights and services trade.

To exploit more fully the opportunities from freer trade, the international policy environment needs to be reinforced. The past quarter-century has seen much progress in strengthening the processes of international consultation and negotiation about global issues. The establishment of the WTO in 1995 has greatly strengthened the permanent institutional mechanisms for the discussion of trade issues and the resolution of disputes. A larger number of non-OECD countries are now persuaded of the importance of trade as a motor of development and several played an important part in bringing the UR negotiations to a successful conclusion. During the seven years following the launch of the Uruguay Round in 1986, over 60 developing countries unilaterally lowered their barriers to imports and 26 have since joined GATT/WTO. Thus, member-ship has grown from 88 in

Table 1.8. **Pre- and Post-Uruguay Round Trade-Weighted Tariffs**
In percentage

Origin	OECD countries			Developing economies			Transition economies		
	Pre-UR	Post-UR	Reduction	Pre-UR	Post-UR	Reduction	Pre-UR	Post-UR	Reduction
OECD countries	5.5	3.0	45	14.9	10.7	28	10.4	7.7	26
Developing economies	6.9	4.8	30	10.0	7.1	29	12.1	8.8	27
Transition economies	5.9	3.6	39	20.8	15.7	25	0.4	0.3	25

Source: OECD.

1985 to 131 today. Moreover, both China and Russia as major players outside the WTO have defined their policies and programmes to gain acceptance into the WTO. Table 1.8 shows the extent of the changes in tariffs resulting from the UR. Tariff barriers between the OECD countries, already close to zero, will fall to a low level on goods from the non-OECD economies. For exports from the OECD to non-OECD economies, the barriers will fall significantly – by an average of 4.2 percentage points in 1999 when the Round is fully implemented.

With the progressive reduction in external trade barriers, further promotion of competition depends critically on the reform of "behind-the-border" barriers – notably, domestic regulation, restrictions on service sector activities, government procurement and subsidies. The further integration of economies facilitated by the removal of these barriers is sometimes referred to as "deep integration" in contrast to the "shallow integration" permitted by removal of border trade barriers. Along with progress on the traditional agenda of tariff cuts, the UR built up momentum to tackle these issues – witness the reform of the Agreement on Technical Barriers to Trade (TBT), plus several new agreements: the General Agreement on Trade in Services (GATS), the Agreement on Trade-related Aspects of Intellectual Property Rights (TRIPS), the Agreement on the Application of Sanitary and Phytosanitary Measures and, subsequently, the Information Technology Agreement. Some of the unresolved sectoral issues left over from the UR are now being tackled or are scheduled for negotiation in the next few years (see Box 1.1).

Although the present time for advancing the global agenda of trade liberalisation looks auspicious, the problems are getting much tougher and more complex. The remaining barriers comprise hard-to-dismantle measures to protect agriculture, textiles and other activities defended by powerful domestic lobbies. Protection from competition through anti-dumping (or contingency protection) usually proves a very expensive and in the long run counterproductive way of preserving jobs. Repeal of contingency protection legislation is unlikely, however, even in a long-term horizon as it enjoys widespread political support. The most practical approach towards lessening its threat (or making it less prone to capture by special interests) may be to introduce a stronger voice for the national interest *via* a greater involvement of competition policy agencies in decisions made in this area.

While contingency protection and hard-core trade restrictions remain significant, the "along-the-border" impediments to trade generally are diminishing. Of greater concern are so-called "behind the frontier" regulations and administrative practices that powerfully impede certain types of trade. Many regulations reduce or eliminate domestic competition and some aim directly at foreign competition. Well-known examples include "buy local" public procurement, monopoly concessions granted to local companies (often public companies) through bans on

Box 1.1.   Unfinished Sectoral Trade Business

Sectoral negotiations left over from the Uruguay Round involved financial services, movement of natural persons, basic telecommunications and maritime transport. An interim agreement on financial services, securing further market access and national treatment commitments in the areas of banking, securities trading and insurance, was accepted by some 30 countries in mid-1995. Negotiations on financial services have resumed and are scheduled to be completed by the end of 1997; the outcome should be further liberalisation, fuller geographical participation and a longer-lasting arrangement.

The negotiations on movement of natural persons were completed in mid-1995. Most countries had made commitments on the movement of natural persons in the Uruguay Round, but nearly all of them were narrow, limited to intra-corporate transferees, and then only to personnel at the managerial level. A few schedules, notably those of Canada and the United States, also contained limited commitments in respect of independent professional service suppliers. Movement of labour is a sensitive issue for all governments, and it is noteworthy that even those countries pressing for better access for different categories of natural persons, such as India and the Philippines, were unwilling to offer much themselves. The post-Uruguay Round negotiations on movement of natural persons brought very little by way of improvements in the schedules of offers, again reflecting the unwillingness of governments to forego control over what is universally seen as a sensitive policy area.

Despite the efforts of negotiators on maritime transport services, it became obvious towards the end of 1993 that a broad-based agreement on maritime services would be impossible. Although negotiations were prolonged until June 1996, it proved impossible to achieve substantial commitments on international shipping, auxiliary services and access and use of port facilities leading to the elimination of existing restrictions within a fixed time frame. A number of countries have traditionally maintained restrictive shipping regimes. Foreign participation in cabotage is prohibited in the United States, for example, and widely restricted in other countries as well. Indeed, cabotage was excluded from the negotiations. Liner conferences have played a prominent role in EU shipping arrangements in various parts of the world. By contrast, the Nordic countries, some EU nations, a number of Asian countries, and some others maintain relatively open maritime regimes. Discussions within the "Negotiating Group on Maritime Transport Services" mainly focused on divergences between the United States and the EU. It has been decided to resume negotiations at the same time as a new round of comprehensive negotiations on liberalisation of services, due to start by the year 2000.

A world-wide trend toward liberalisation in the telecommunications sector is clearly discernible. Globalisation of economic activity has increased the importance of telecommunications as a production input, making firms much more sensitive to competitive disadvantages arising from poor or costly services. This has mobilised powerful private sector constituencies in many countries to push governments to liberalise and eliminate or dilute telecommunications monopolies. These pressures contributed to a successful completion of the WTO negotiations on basic telecommunications, which had been carried over inconclusively from the Uruguay Round. On 15 February 1997, 69 governments made market access commitments under the General Agreement on Trade in Services (GATS). Many of these governments also accepted a set of multilaterally negotiated regulatory principles, designed to ensure that commitments to market opening cannot be frustrated by dominant incumbent suppliers. The results of these negotiations, which are scheduled to enter into force in 1998, have been widely hailed as a significant contribution to reform in the telecommunications sector. Several governments have accelerated their liberalisation plans in the context of the GATS negotiations. Others have undertaken legal guarantees to introduce competition into their markets within a specified time frame. Overall, this is the most significant package of results at a sectoral level to have been negotiated under the auspices of GATS.

the entry of other potential players (power, postal services, telecommunications, tobacco and alcoholic beverage sales are examples commonly found in the OECD), and regulations on professional services that mandate local presence, require local professional qualifications, restrict the establishment of foreign firms, or require payment of services according to standardised fees.

The non-OECD countries also use many of the same instruments. One example is the cosseting of fledgling national car industries in some Asian countries where restrictions are imposed to reduce foreign competition. Sometimes the use of protection takes on a rather comprehensive form as when designated priority sectors and industries receive active support through special low-cost credit arrangements, tax incentives, or preferential access to foreign exchange for inputs and investment goods or public infrastructure. Most governments, including OECD governments, use subsidies to industry as a policy instrument. Often spurred by intense lobbying from business interests and trade unions, many subsidies aim to help local firms and industries retain or restore competitiveness. One example of an effort to eliminate subsidies is the Ship-building Agreement recently concluded under the aegis of the OECD. Initially involving the European Community, the Republic of Korea, Japan, Norway and the United States (which has not yet ratified it), it is expected to attract other shipbuilding countries to accede and accept the same disciplines.

As discussed in Chapter 3, large benefits, mainly in terms of greater price stability, higher productivity and living standards, can be achieved by stimulating more competition in domestic markets through regulatory reform, including deregulation. Changing the rules to facilitate new local entrants is a part of the process, but in markets dominated by large players international competition plays a vital role. Indeed, a strong complementarity between competition policy and trade and investment policy has become increasingly recognised as a key element in the new trade agenda. The growing interest in competition law and practice at the international level in part reflects these concerns: thus Chapter 15 of the North American Free Trade Agreement (NAFTA) explicitly recognised the importance of competition policy, and Mexico took steps prior to implementation of the Agreement to create a competition law. Competition policies, however, tend to have a rather limited scope and many competition-inhibiting policies (for instance public procurement rules) tend to fall outside the jurisdiction of the competition authority. The strengthening of competition policy and international agreements or understandings relating to it likely will remain high on the policy agenda.

Other interactions occur between trade policy and the regulatory environment. Domestic regulations can, intentionally or not, undo or neutralise commitments undertaken in other policy domains, including trade liberalisa-tion. Divergent preferences in domestic policy areas such as environmental quality and social protection may lead to different regulations and financial charges which can have an impact on relative competitive positions. Some-times, as in the discussion of intellectual property rights and environmental issues, the trade policy dimension is associated primarily with the enforce-ment of agreements, as the threat of denial of trade benefits may appear to offer an effective means of securing other policy objectives. Thus, at a time when many of the traditional arguments for protection have been largely dis-counted (on practical grounds, if not in theory), other kinds of justification are replacing them. In these cases, however, the traditional argument is stood on its head: the threat of trade sanctions is a powerful weapon precisely because the benefits of trade are so valuable. As a rule, trade measures/restraints should not be used to achieve what are essentially non-trade-related domestic policy objectives. They should only be used in accordance with applicable internationally-agreed rules, which take account of any trade-distorting effects as well as any other agreed global policy objectives where the use of such measures is considered to be appropriate (for example, the use of trade measures under multilateral environmental agreements).

Strengthening international accountability

Recent World Trade Organisation (WTO) and other agreements mark considerable progress in strengthening the international accountability of national regulatory regimes. Globalisation and growing interdependence will surely move international negotiation further in this direction. In general, the objective is to safeguard the right of governments to pursue legitimate public policy objectives – for example, in regard to social safeguards – while denying or minimising the use of policy instruments that serve to neutralise pre-existing market access commitments and frustrate the momentum towards open, competitive trade. The challenge – a major one – is to extend the beginnings made under existing agreements to a larger field of activities.

One approach, embodied in the main WTO agreements, involves government commitments concerning their domestic regulatory regimes: non-discrimination; an obligation to give reasons for regulating; transparency; and the avoidance of unnecessary trade restrictiveness. The approach maximises the flexibility of governments to define the objectives of regulatory interventions, and provides a large element of flexibility in the manner of achieving them. The WTO rules based on these principles constitute the most significant set of international commitments in the field of regulation for most countries, especially non-OECD countries.

An additional commitment, though one rarely sought, recognises an international obligation to enforce domestic regulations. With such a commitment, lax enforcement could be challenged and become the grounds for invoking dispute settlement procedures. Some elements of the TRIPs agreement have such requirements. A clearer example occurs in the 1994 North American Agreement on Labour Co-operation (NAALC), a supplementary agreement to the North American Free Trade Agreement (NAFTA). In essence, the NAALC sets up co-operative machinery in matters of labour policy, the centrepiece being the right of a Member to challenge another on the enforcement of the latter's own labour laws. Remedies in the face of non-compliance include, ultimately, retaliation through trade restrictions.

Convergence of domestic laws and regulations can be achieved through harmonisation of national regulatory frameworks, mutual recognition agreements (MRAs), or *de facto* competition among regulatory systems. In any case, governments face pressures to preserve if not enhance the competitive positions of their business and labour interests. Their efforts to fulfil these expectations will continue as a significant cause of friction at the international level and managing it will remain a pressing challenge for international trade-related policy. The debate on labour standards highlights the complex issues involved (see Box 1.2).

Another approach that seeks to avert some of the perceived ills of regulatory diversity across jurisdictions involves mutual recognition agreements (MRAs). These agreements are most feasible where national regulatory regimes and institutional capabilities are already similar – a situation most prevalent among countries at comparable income and development levels. The most extensive experience is that of the EU where the rather substantial degree of free movement in goods and (to a lesser degree) services has resulted from many years of government negotiations (plus important interventions from the EU judiciary branch). The main virtue of MRAs from a market access perspective is that they typically exempt foreign suppliers from the double administrative burden of proving their goods meet the importing country's standards if they already meet the exporting country's standards. MRAs can apply both to the content of regulations and standards or (more often) to their enforcement (*e.g.* testing and conformity assessment for products, professional licensing, financial market supervision). Thus far, however, MRAs have proven to be a resource- and time-intensive method of dealing with the market access effects of regulatory heterogeneity and concerns have been raised among some segments of public opinion about infringement of national sovereignty. The difficulties that the practice of mutual recognition have revealed "on the ground" confirm the importance of reinforcing the multilateral system's signalling functions and instruments. In general, it is advisable to define a framework of minimum criteria to ensure that domestic regulation is consistent with promoting greater competition and enhancing market access. From the perspective of an individual country, one potentially cost-effective approach is to rely on international standards, where they exist, in designing new domestic standards and regulations.

International, regional and other institutions

While the WTO has been and will continue to be the central institution in promoting and negotiating multilateral agreements, difficulties impede both consensus among the large and economically disparate WTO membership and management of more and more complex structures, including the disputes settlement procedures. Regional institutions may enable trade barriers to be reduced faster and allow more progress to be made on the behind-the-border trade issues, with bargaining among a small group of like-minded countries. The EU provides a prominent example (see Box 1.3). The NAFTA (while not intended to be as all-encompassing as the EU) also embraces issues beyond trade barriers in the form of side-agreements on the environment and labour standards. Other regional associations which deal with a wide range of trade-related issues include ASEAN and Mercosur.

Using regional agreements as a complement to the multilateral approach to lowering trade barriers may produce quicker and more comprehensive results applicable to trade between regional partners. There is a well-known risk, however, of disfavouring lower-cost outside suppliers against higher-cost insiders. The EU's agricultural policy and its rather liberal use of Community contingency protection legislation exemplify this tendency. Also, when powerful interests coalesce around regional trade barriers, they may constitute potent opposition to the extension of the arrangement to new partner-members.

The OECD as an organisation plays a role in the international effort to secure trade policy objectives through its work in furthering the understanding of the issues and promotion of consensus in the approaches of the Member governments. The OECD can help in the pre-negotiation phase through the informal exchange of policy options and ideas among Members, and by carrying out relevant analysis and developing policy recommendations. The interlocking system of working parties facilitates the pursuit of a wide range of the issues through a multidisciplinary review process so that the trade aspect can be considered along with other concerns. Through its outreach programmes, OECD has formal and informal contacts with many officials in major non-OECD economies and the periodic interchange through seminars and other fora allows for a sampling of opinion from outside the OECD Membership. As widening the application of policy consensus (and occasional formal agreements), first arrived at among the Membership, becomes a more important aspect of the work, consideration should be given to arrangements for strengthening the consultative channels and modalities of dialogue with non-OECD economies.

1.3. Towards Global Financial Integration

The benefits of global capital mobility result from a better allocation of world savings to the most productive investment opportunities and the possibility to maintain consumption in the event of adverse shocks and sustain consumption levels of future pensioners following the prior build-up of financial assets abroad. These benefits apply particularly in the interaction between the capital-rich, moderately-growing and ageing OECD economies and the capital-poor, fast-growing and (still) young emerging ones. Multinational corporations or portfolio investors from OECD countries have the prospect of raising returns (higher profits, dividend payments and interest income) through increasing their exposure in high-growth emerging economies. For the increasingly service-oriented economies of OECD countries, FDI in non-OECD economies represents an important means of exploiting their comparative advantage, since many services remain nontradable. Moreover, in the tradables sector, high-wage jobs are often consolidated by outsourcing low-wage components through foreign direct investment.

The emerging markets can benefit from FDI in several ways. FDI involves a transfer of technology and managerial know-how; it often facilitates the growth of a country's exports by securing access to world markets; it stimulates recipient countries' investment (through local outsourcing and positive technology spill-overs), and it can enhance competition. Recent empirical work has found that under certain conditions foreign direct investment has a larger impact on growth than other types of capital inflows. The preconditions are that a) economic distortions, and in particular tariffs and sectoral subsidies, must have been removed in host economies, so as to avoid directing FDI into inefficient sectors; and b) host countries must have a minimum threshold stock of human capital to benefit from embodied transfer of technology.

Greater diversification of OECD investment into non-member capital markets offers the prospect of higher risk-adjusted returns. This may hold part of a solution to the fiscal and financial problems looming on the horizon as OECD populations grow old. Many types of asset holders in OECD countries could benefit from these diversification gains (e.g., firms, households, banks), but they may be of particular interest to institutional investors such as pension and investment funds and insurance companies. Such institutional assets have grown dramatically over the past decade and this trend will continue as the baby boom generation enters the period in its life cycle of saving at higher rates from increasing incomes and as public pension systems come under growing stress from higher old-age dependency. Meanwhile, in the non-OECD area, labour force growth will require higher investment to turn potential labour supply into a productive workforce. While lower fertility rates in emerging economies will spur local savings, part of the growing capital demand will likely be financed by OECD retirement savings (as well as by foreign direct investment).

The diversification gains for OECD investors would occur even if there were no increase in net financial flows to emerging markets. Since, as explained below, emerging market investors may also gain from greater diversification into OECD markets, reverse flows may to some extent counterbalance gross outflows from the OECD area. Moreover, it is unlikely that net inflows to emerging markets would increase significantly over the long run since non-OECD economies have historically relied overwhelmingly on domestic savings to finance investment needs, and this is unlikely to change in the future (see Chapter 2 for further discussion).

The case for mutual benefits arising from the global diversification of portfolios is nowhere stronger than for funded retirement savings. While unfunded (pay-as-you-go) pension schemes are locked into the ageing economy, fully funded pension schemes would not escape demographic pressures if their assets were to remain invested in ageing countries alone. Indeed, when the baby boom generation starts to draw on the funded pension schemes, the impact of that decumulation on local asset prices and thus on pension benefits might be negative. The diversification of OECD pension assets into the non-OECD stock markets provides the prospect of higher expected return for a given level of risk or, put alternatively, lower risk by eliminating non-systemic volatility without sacrificing expected return. It is less the superior growth performance of the non-OECD area than the low correlation of returns generated by the emerging stock markets with those of the OECD stock markets that governs this expectation. The correlation between returns on OECD and emerging stock markets will remain low even when diversification gains are seriously exploited. Differences between the two areas with respect to the exposure to country-specific shocks, the stage of economic and demographic maturity and the (lack of) harmonisation of economic policies suggest that the diversification gains for OECD pension assets will not disappear quickly. The benefits of global portfolio diversification also apply to emerging country pension assets as they could diversify away some of the risks stemming from high exposure to shocks in their own countries by investing a portion of their pension assets in OECD countries.

Table 1.9. **The home-asset preference in funded pension assets**

	1990	1995e
Total pension assets, bn $		
OECD	4 813	7 865
Non-OECD	109	311
Home-asset share, % of assets[a]		
OECD pension assets	92.8	88.9
Non-OECD pension assets[b]	100.0	99.3

e   Estimate.
a)   Home-assets share refers only to the share of assets invested in the home country of the investor.
b)   Excludes Hong Kong where the foreign asset share is 60 per cent.
Source: InterSec Research Company.

Table 1.9 documents the strong growth in OECD and non-OECD pension assets, the most important institutional vehicle for portfolio investments (equities and bonds). The Figure also shows that these are heavily invested in home assets (defined as assets held in the home country of the investor only), though the home bias in OECD assets has been reduced during the 1990s, including through investment into emerging markets. This latter trend should continue over the next 25 years, because the emerging markets still offer much unexploited potential to improve the risk-adjusted returns of OECD pension assets.

Realising benefits from global capital mobility will require further liberalisation of regulations on capital movements in both OECD and non-OECD countries, as well as an adaptation of multilateral rules of the game to secure international investment. In the past decades, progress in freeing international capital markets has mostly occurred through liberalisation of capital controls among the OECD countries and largely under OECD auspices. The non-OECD economies have shown growing interest in recent years in attracting private international capital and have taken measures to reap the potential gains from capital and financial market liberalisation. In many of those countries, however, there is still need for measures to increase competition in their banking and financial sectors, subject to essential prudential safeguards.

Although restrictions on capital movement have been almost entirely eliminated in the OECD area, certain types of institutional investors, pension funds and life insurance companies in particular, still face important regulatory barriers on their capacity to invest abroad. The challenge for regulators in OECD countries is to free institutional assets so that they will be able to seek the best mix of risk and return and realise the mutual benefits stemming from shifting OECD pension assets to emerging markets. At the same time, governments have a legitimate interest in close supervision of pension funds, given likely pressures on them to compensate losers in the event of a major bankruptcy. Reduction of the excessive home bias of OECD pension assets would imply moving away from administratively set asset allocation rules to some more general principles of prudence in managing portfolios. A helpful step would be an early application of the discipline of the OECD Codes of Liberalisation to portfolio investment abroad by insurance companies and private pension funds. An adequate representation of the emerging stock markets in the performance benchmarks relevant to the pension industry would also help.

In non-OECD economies, the reform agenda is bigger. Regulations to discourage capital outflows are far more prevalent in non-OECD countries, and some of these countries also have concerns about excessive short-term inflows. These worries are motivated either by the macroeconomic implications of capital inflows on real exchange rates, external debt and deficit levels or by their intermediation through ill-supervised banking systems. Many non-OECD economies still have excessive state intervention in the banking system, illiquid and poorly regulated stock-markets and over-regulated institutional investors. Vested interests may agitate against FDI in fear of intensified domestic competition in manufacturing and/or in financial services. Again, such concerns tend to motivate a panoply of policy measures that dampen the free movement of capital across borders.

The challenge to policy makers in the non-OECD countries is to draw up a comprehensive programme for the removal of capital controls, the liberalisation of market access and domestic regulatory reform, without compromising financial stability (see Box 1.4). Authorities can best ensure that financial market evolution will sustain and strengthen financial stability by expeditious implementation of a coherent strategy for financial liberalisation. The transition to liberalised capital flows necessitates a careful examination of the timing and sequencing of reforms, as they have economy-wide ramifications. When a country is visibly engaged in promising economic reform, investors try to get a claim on the economy. Such a stock adjustment, however, falls on a very small asset base and shallow financial markets relative to OECD assets. While the stock adjustment may soon change profitability enough to discourage additional inflows into the emerging economy, the problem is in the orders of magnitude and the ability to co-ordinate the impact of capital flows. Governments and central banks should thus care about the sustainability of capital flows which their economies can tap abroad. A full analysis of the likely effects and sustainability of liberalisation – and therefore the advisability at any moment in time of doing it – needs to take into account the macroeconomic policy framework, the state of the financial system, and the ability of product and labour markets to adjust to domestic and external financial shocks. In recognition of these problems, new OECD Members have been permitted to lodge substantial reservations under the Codes, primarily in respect of short-term capital inflows.

The aftermath of the Mexican financial crisis of December 1994 has enlivened the concern that contagion effects towards other emerging markets might result in a global financial crisis. Apart from the potential damage done by a systemic financial crisis on a global scale, contagion effects are of concern for both OECD-based investors and developing-country governments. From the investor's point of view, the benefits of international portfolio diversification shrink if returns to emerging stock markets are driven predominantly by systemic factors external to these markets themselves, because global diversification can reduce only non-systemic risk. From the perspective of policymakers in recipient countries, contagion effects imply costly capital-flow reversals caused by factors outside their control, reducing the potential benefits of financial opening. As the ongoing process of financial integration reaches more emerging markets and they come to depend increasingly on private capital flows, the impact on global financial stability will need to be addressed.

Further progress with financial liberalisation will also require an intensification and upgrading of surveillance and the provision of adequate technical assistance. Surveillance will be of particular importance for those countries which need to upgrade significantly their financial structure and their regulatory/supervisory frameworks in order to be able to engage in, and reap the benefits of, liberalisation. Over the past decade, substantial efforts have been made to establish international rules of the game in banking and finance, including supervisory principles and standards through the work of the Basle Committee on Banking Supervision and the International Organisation of Securities Commissions. These efforts will need to be sustained and accelerated in the years ahead to cope with both the increasing complexity of financial business and the expanding range of countries and institutions operating in the global market.

The Multilateral Agreement on Investment (MAI)

Foreign investors still encounter investment barriers, discriminatory treatment and legal and regulatory uncertainties. National treatment and most favoured nation treatment are still fairly uncommon in many countries. Even privatisation which has been a core element of structural reforms since the early 1990s has not been exempted from various restrictions *vis-à-vis* foreign investors. Moreover, with more than thousand existing unilateral, bilateral, regional and sectoral agreements to date, the multiplicity of channels, through which foreign investment liberalisation has been achieved, has created a high degree of confusion concerning enforceable rules in various situations. This has created a case for establishing a multilateral regulatory framework that would pull together under one single instrument the disciplines of national treatment and most favoured nation treatment.

The Uruguay Round did address some trade-related investment issues in the successfully concluded agreements on TRIMs, TRIPs and GATS. Opposition to a broad-based negotiation on investment in the Uruguay Round was nevertheless strong enough to prevent more than a narrow negotiating mandate for TRIMs. The UR TRIMs Agreement essentially reaffirms GATT rules on national treatment and on the prohibition of quantitative restrictions. It singles out two measures – local content requirements and trade balancing requirements – as discrimination against foreign investors. It also identifies as illegal quantitative restrictions, foreign exchange balancing requirements, and domestic sales requirements. The Agreement requires that WTO-inconsistent TRIMs be phased out, and that no new WTO-inconsistent TRIMs be introduced during the phase-out period. Industrial countries must complete the phase-out within two years, developing countries within five years, and least developed countries within seven years. These measures represent important steps in the development of international discipline, but they address to only a limited extent the investment concerns that still hinder the flow of capital.

When successfully completed, the Multilateral Agreement on Investment (MAI) will provide for a high standard of liberalisation of investment regimes, a level playing field for international investors and an effective dispute settlement mechanism. It will provide a benchmark against which potential investors can assess the openness and legal security offered by countries as investment locations (see Box 1.5). The ultimate aim is to create a more favourable investment environment for enterprises confronted with the challenge of globalisation and thereby encourage investment flows. The MAI will be a free-standing treaty; that is, although the MAI is being negotiated in the OECD, it will not be an OECD instrument. Instead, it will be open to accession by interested non-OECD economies. Signing-up to the MAI will indicate to investors that the country concerned subscribes to the highest standards in market access, legal protection and equitable treatment. For non-OECD economies that are also a source of outward investment, the MAI will offer the additional attraction of assuring market access and legal protection for investment into other countries party to the agreement.

Tax linkages: emerging challenges and opportunities

Globalisation has had a major impact on the international tax environment. The liberalisation and integration of national capital and financial markets have made particular segments of national tax bases increasingly mobile. The rapid expansion of commerce over global information infrastructures, notably in service sector activities, has speeded up the breaking down of national boundaries. The anonymity and "virtuality" built into the Internet and other networks has weakened the linkage between the place where services are performed and the place they are consumed and has made it increasingly difficult to identify particular transactions and individual taxpayers.

As other obstacles to the free flow of capital have been dismantled, business international financing and investment decisions have become more sensitive to tax differentials. Tax competition occurs as soon as the tax structures of two countries differ. This concept is more commonly associated, however, with the deliberate use of tax incentives or, as in recent years, of preferential tax regimes to attract foreign direct investment and financial activities.

Increasing globalisation and interdependence have increased opportunities for tax avoidance and evasion, reduced the feasibility of high tax rates on capital

Box 1.5. Main features of the Multilateral Agreement on Investment (MAI)

The MAI will provide broad coverage through a comprehensive asset-based definition of investment applying to all economic sectors. The draft definition of "investor" includes a natural person, corporation, trust, partnership, sole proprietorship, joint venture, association or organisation. The draft definition of "investment" includes an enterprise, shares, stocks or other forms of equity participation, bonds, debentures, loans, rights under contracts, claims to money, intellectual property rights, construction or management contracts, production or revenue-sharing contracts, and real estate.

Investment protection. The MAI provisions are largely based on the principles enshrined in bilateral investment protection treaties: *a*) the general treatment of the investor and the investment, *b*) expropriation and compensation, *c*) protection from strife, *d*) transfer of funds, *e*) subrogation, and *f*) protection of investor rights arising from investment agreements between the investor and the host country.

The treatment of investors and their investments will be based on *national treatment* and *most favoured nation treatment*. These principles will apply to both the "establishment phase" and "post-establishment" phase. They would forbid *de facto* and *de jure* discrimination. These principles are complemented by a transparency provision concerning the publication or the public availability of laws, regulations, procedures and administrative rulings, and judicial decisions of general application pertaining to foreign investment.

National treatment and most favoured nation treatment provisions are the basic treatment standards. Additional provisions clarify the application of these obligations in given situations or circumstances, or add to the level of openness of investment foreseen by them. Six *special topics* have been identified: key personnel, performance requirements, investment incentives, privatisation, monopolies/state enterprises, concessions and, finally, corporate practices.

Dispute settlement. The credibility of the MAI will be assured by binding international arbitration of investment disputes both *a*) between states and *b*) between an investor and a participating state. The mechanism for settling state-to-state disputes would follow the WTO precedent which makes the admissibility of an issue in arbitration depend on its having been raised for resolution through consultation. Any dispute between contracting parties which has not been resolved by a requested consultation could be submitted to an *ad hoc* MAI arbitral Panel. Arbitral awards would be considered final and binding upon the contracting parties to the arbitral proceedings.

income, contributed to the erosion of the tax base in many countries and made it virtually impossible for countries to rely solely on domestic measures to determine the scope of and to protect their tax bases. Consequently, the importance of international considerations in the determination of national tax policies is increasing. The possibilities for tax planning have also expanded, which in turn has raised the potential for conflicts between tax administrations of different countries and between national tax administrations and taxpayers. As an inevitable consequence, governments of both developed and developing countries have become more willing to seek international co-operation to ensure that their domestic tax systems work in the ways intended.

The OECD has responded to the rapid globalisation of the world economy by intensifying work on developing truly global principles and rules in the fields of tax treaties, transfer pricing and tax avoidance. The most important achievement has been the development and adoption of the OECD *Model Tax Convention on Income and Capital*. As a result of the widespread use of the Model Convention, bilateral tax treaties between developed and developing countries as well as tax treaties between developing countries tend to follow the pattern of the Model and include similar provisions to a large extent.

To encourage the use of the Model Tax Convention among non-OECD countries and to ensure that the Model Convention is interpreted and applied uniformly in both Member and non-OECD countries, the OECD has opened up a dialogue in this field with more than 50 non-OECD countries. The dialogue with non-OECD countries has been extended to encompass the OECD Guidelines on Transfer Pricing adopted in 1995. To counter the increasing possibilities for international tax avoidance and evasion, the dialogue aims to encourage non-OECD countries to adopt the OECD manuals and guidelines on exchange of information between tax authorities and to identify legal barriers and practical obstacles to a more effective exchange of information, including examining ways to remove them. It also seeks new ways to pool information.

In May 1996 the OECD Ministerial decided to focus on harmful tax competition and propose measures to counter the harmful impact of tax competition in the financial and other services sectors. By identifying tax regimes which are particularly damaging, the aim is to recommend ways in which countries, acting individually or collectively, can best address the problems presented to them by countries operating particularly harmful regimes within or outside the OECD area. Work has begun at the OECD on how to avoid potential frictions between MAI obligations and tax considerations. Preliminary discussions have also been held on issues of extra-territoriality, such as conflicting requirements that investors or investments may face when operating in more than one state.

1.4. Environmental Issues

The environmental implications of globalisation and closer linkages between OECD countries and non-OECD economies can be both positive and negative, depending on the pace and direction of economic growth and the robustness of the environmental policy frameworks established in both groups of countries. With appropriate environmental policies in place, increased trade and investment linkages have the potential to promote a more efficient and less environmentally-damaging pattern of economic development. These outcomes could be achieved in several ways: by promoting more efficient use of raw material and energy inputs through the removal of subsidies; through shifts in demand and production patterns towards less material- and energy-intensive goods and services, thereby decoupling economic growth from pollution generation; through the development and diffusion of cleaner technologies; by reducing poverty and its associated environmental effects in the major developing economies; and by generating additional wealth which could help finance environmental improvement.

Even if all environmental externalities were internalised – which is far from the case at present – globalisation would still likely shift pollution and resource-intensive production to countries with comparative advantages in assimilative capacity and resource endowments. Trade and investment liberalisation may result in more efficient resource usage and positive welfare effects globally; but at the same time they are likely to induce an uneven distribution of environmental changes. In many cases, environmental pressures would intensify in the non-OECD economies, though there may also be increased pressures in OECD countries.

Thus far, it is largely in OECD countries that dematerialisation and decoupling of economic growth from pollution have occurred; among developing countries, only those approaching OECD income levels and economic structures show similar patterns, while those at an earlier stage of rapid industrialisation often witness rapid pollution growth. Some forms of pollution may exhibit an inverted-U curve relationship with economic development, as industrialisation and agricultural modernisation initially result in increased pollution and resource use before changes in economic structure, societal preferences and public policies reverse these trends. How the pollution profile evolves will depend, however, on a combination of factors – scale, structure, technology and policy. While scale effects (growing production and pollution volumes) may dominate for some time, historical experience suggests that with changes in the composition of economic activity (notably towards services) pollution-intensity of output will decline. Moreover, linkage-intensive development should facilitate the adoption of more advanced (which often implies cleaner) technologies. Finally, policy itself is endogenous, responding to domestic and international pressures for environmental improvements. As countries grow richer, people's preferences and willingness to pay for environmental quality strengthen.

Globalisation and the economic growth it fosters can have an impact on a number of environmental dimensions. Closer linkages may amplify and/or reorient existing environmental pressures. The projected shift in economic weight from OECD countries to the non-OECD economies, as well as continued population growth in the latter, means that they will make an increasingly significant contribution to regional and global environmental problems. While the material and pollution intensity of OECD economies may be decreasing, their "ecological footprints" – the demands placed on the environments in other countries – may be increasing, calling into question the equity and sustainability of current global patterns of production and consumption. The Worldwatch Institute has suggested in its 1997 *State of the World* report that eight nations – the E8 – will disproportionately shape global environmental trends: Brazil, China, Germany, India, Indonesia, Japan, Russia and the United States (see Table 1.10). The industrial countries of this group shape global trends through their economic strength, their high levels of consumption and their dominance of technology. The developing countries' influence stems from their large populations, their rapid economic development and their rich biodiversity (though on this point some very small countries like Madagascar carry inordinate weight). Together they account for more than half of the world's population, its economic output, its carbon emissions and its forests.

Some of the key global and transboundary environmental issues involving the non-OECD economies and, more specifically, the Big Five are briefly outlined below, drawing extensively on the 1997 *Global Environmental Outlook* of the United Nations Environment Programme (UNEP).

Carbon Dioxide Emissions: Given their relatively high GDP growth and the relatively high energy-intensity and CO_2-intensity of that growth (compared to OECD countries) (see Figure 1.9), the non-OECD countries and, in particular the Big Five, will be major contributors to global CO_2 emissions in the future. The first

Table 1.10. **Eight environmentally important countries**
Per cent

	Share of world population	Share of gross world product	Share of world carbon emissions	Share of world forest area	Share of flowering plant species
	1996	1994	1995	1990	1990[a]
United States	5	26	23	6	8
Russian Federation	3	2	7	21	9
Japan	2	17	5	0.7	2
Germany	1	8	4	0.3	1
China	21	2	13	4	12
India	17	1	4	2	6
Indonesia	4	0.7	1	3	8
Brazil	3	2	1	16	22
Total	**56**	**59**	**59**	**53**	..

a) Based on a total of 250 000 known species. Total could not be calculated due to overlap in species among countries.
Source: Worldwatch Institute (1997), *State of the World 1997.* W.W. Norton and Co., New York.

◆ Figure I.9. **CO_2 emissions intensity[1]: 1992**

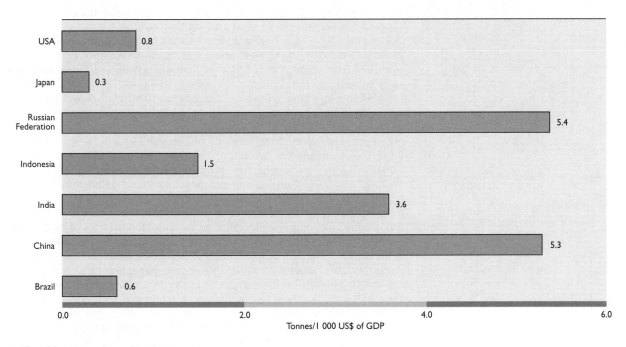

Tonnes/1 000 US$ of GDP

1. Total CO_2 emissions from industrial processes.
Source: World Resources Institute (1996), World Resources 1996-97; World Bank (1994), World Development Report 1994.

half of the 1990s provides some indication of what might be expected if high growth rates are sustained and policies remain unchanged. From 1990 to 1994, carbon emissions rose by 13 per cent in China, 15.8 per cent in Brazil, and 23.5 per cent in India.

Transboundary Air Pollution: Acid rain is an emerging problem in Asia-Pacific and parts of Latin America. An estimated 38 million tons of SO_2 were emitted in 22 Asian countries in 1990, with about 78 per cent of this total originating in North-East Asia. In China, SO_2 emissions increased from 15.2 million tons in 1985 to 18.0 million tons in 1993. Fly ash associated with thermal power generation also contributes to transboundary air pollution through the release of suspended particulates: India generates an estimated 35-40 million tons of fly ash annually but re-uses only 2-3 per cent.

Damage to the Ozone Layer: By 1995 world-wide production of the most widely used ozone depleting substances, CFCs, had dropped 76 per cent from its peak in 1988. At the beginning of 1996, industrialised countries were required to stop producing and importing CFCs for domestic use with the exception of some "essential uses". There is a lengthy lag, however, between the emissions decline and a full recovery of the ozone layer, expected to occur about 2045 if all countries comply with the Montreal Protocol. Cases of non-compliance and growth in illegal trade in CFCs present emerging problems: it has been suggested that in late 1995 about a fifth of the CFCs in use world-wide were illegally traded. As Article 5 parties to the Montreal Protocol, Brazil, China, India and Indonesia have until 2010 to phase out CFCs. Several have indicated their intention to achieve this goal before then: *e.g.*, Indonesia by 1997, Brazil by 2001.

Fisheries: More than 60 per cent of the world's marine fisheries are heavily exploited. OECD countries and the Big Five host some of the largest fishing fleets: in 1993 China was the most important fishing nation with a total catch of 17.6 million tonnes (Mt) followed by Japan (8.5 Mt) in second place, the USA (5.9 Mt) in fifth and Russia (4.5 Mt), India (4.2 Mt) and Indonesia (3.6 Mt) in the sixth through eighth places. FAO projects that demand for fish products will rise 26 per cent between 1993 and 2010. Access to fish stocks is already a source of tension between countries in some regions. While a growing share of the world's fish consumption will be supplied from aquaculture, this source would not likely compensate for a collapse of stocks in several major fisheries. Moreover, experience with shrimp cultivation suggests that the input-intensive practices employed in many areas of south-east Asia may themselves be unsustainable.

Forests and Deforestation: The world's forests and wooded land declined by 2 per cent in the 1980s. While the forest area in industrialised countries remained largely unchanged, the natural forest cover in developing countries declined 8 per cent. Brazil, China and India had annual deforestation rates of 0.7 per cent while Indonesia's rate was higher at 1.1 per cent. The problem of deforestation is by no means new, but because in recent decades much of it has occurred in tropical rainforests that are major repositories of biodiversity particular concerns have arisen within both the environmental and scientific communities. The International Tropical Timber Organisation has promoted voluntary guidelines for sustainable forest management as a means of pre-empting mandatory restrictions. Some countries have imposed logging or log export bans, but these have not proved very effective. Multilateral measures might include the incorporation of incentives for the conservation and cultivation of forests into international environmental agreements – *e.g.* in follow-on agreements to the Framework Convention on Climate Change as one means of earning carbon credits that can then be traded, or perhaps as a feature of the biodiversity convention.

Biodiversity: Latin America and Asia-Pacific together account for 80 per cent of the ecological megadiversity countries of the world. Habitat loss and fragmentation, the lack of biological corridors and the decline in biodiversity outside protected areas constitute the principal threats to overall biodiversity. At current rates the conversion and deforestation of tropical and dry forests in Latin America may destroy 100 000-450 000 species within the next 40 years; many of these species have not yet been inventoried or described adequately. A trend towards reliance on a smaller number of varieties for food production may also pose threats to biodiversity: by 2005, India is expected to produce 75 per cent of its rice from just 10 varieties compared with the 30 000 varieties traditionally cultivated. In Indonesia, 1 500 varieties of rice disappeared during the period 1975-1990. This concern needs to be set against the potential for production gains from reliance on a few high quality cultivars – witness the European and US experience.

The OECD countries have made substantial progress on their own domestic environmental agendas over the past 25 years, although the remaining challenges far outweigh the accomplishments. With rapid economic development fostered by globalisation, many non-OECD countries may be able to do the same. Still, substantial uncertainty remains about the impact further globalisation may have on the global environment. The impact of future world economic growth on greenhouse gas emissions is discussed in the next chapter, while policy implications are addressed in Chapter 3.

CHAPTER 2.   THE WORLD ECONOMY IN 2020

To enlarge the opportunities for mutual gains from globalisation for OECD and 5 non-OECD countries alike, further progress will be needed with trade and financial liberalisation as well as with domestic reform, including privatisation and deregulation of markets. Considerations will also have to be given to the environmental dimension of globalisation, and more particularly, to the framework of policies needed to ensure that the rapid growth of world output expected to result from accelerated globalisation is environmentally sustainable.

The historic coincidence of interest between OECD countries and non-OECD economies in creating a truly global world economy has opened up a window of opportunity for all countries to speed up the reform process and to show greater resolve in overcoming the resistance to required changes and necessary adaptations. Anticipating such a cause of action and events leads to the vision that the move towards a "New Global Age" could be completed in less than a quarter century with all artificial barriers to trade and exchange removed, and free cross-boarder flows of goods, services, capital and technical know-how at low or close to zero cost. This vision encompasses the entire community of nations, more and more closely bound together by growing economic interdependance, sharing a commitment to a multilateral system of rules-based competition and governance institutions, and united in their common concern to safeguard the earth's natural wealth and global environment for the benefit of present and future generations.

The following sections of this chapter explore prospects for the world economy to the year 2020 under different policy assumptions: a fast and a slow track reform and adjustment scenario, (a "high-performance" and a "business-as-usual" scenario), labelled henceforth high-growth (HG) and low-growth (LG) scenarios respectively, in accordance with projected outcomes. Constructing plausible scenarios of global development involves quite formidable problems even when the timeframe is much shorter. The value of scenario analysis does not lie in its power to predict future economic conditions or events with accuracy, but in the insights it affords about the weight of various driving forces that might influence global outcomes. The use of a consistent modelling framework, including macro models and applied general equilibrium (GE) models that have been designed and estimated as part of this study, permits the exploration of impacts from different policy and growth scenarios on trade and production patterns, on food and energy markets, and on the global environment.

The GDP growth rates for particular countries or regions reflected in the two scenarios do not represent forecasts, nor are they to be construed as setting upper or lower bounds on the growth possibilities. Just as economic performance could turn out much better than predicted in the HG scenario, most likely to occur if reforms and adjustments to the "New Global Age" proceed faster than assumed, conversely a much worse performance than shown in the LG scenario for individual countries and the world as a whole could result from major policy reversals. One could envisage lower growth scenarios if, for example *a*) OECD countries cannot successfully adjust their industrial and employment structures to accommodate technical change and shifting comparative advantage, resulting in a resurgence of protectionism; *b*) domestic policy failures occur in some of the large non-OECD economies; or *c*) the global environment were to experience rapid and severe deterioration through, for example, the collapse of global fisheries, agricultural productivity declines, and/or more frequent and severe natural disasters.

The major difference between the two growth scenarios resides in assumptions about progress with policy reforms (see Box 2.1). In the HG scenario, governments are assumed to make substantial further progress with global trade and investment liberalisation and with domestic policy reforms, in Member and non-OECD countries alike. The LG scenario assumes less trade and investment liberalisation and slower progress on domestic policy reforms, especially in the areas of fiscal consolidation, removal of domestic subsidies and structural policies.

2.1. Global Growth Prospects

Under the HG scenario, assuming OECD countries can implement the main parts of their policy agenda successfully, the long-term productivity prospects and the labour market outlook are favourable with GDP growth roughly the same rate as in the past 25 years (i.e., 2.9 per cent per annum, see Figure 2.1). GDP per capita would rise more quickly due to slowing population growth. However, slow progress on policy reforms, when added to the effects of population ageing, could cause a progressive slowing of OECD growth rates to 1.7 per cent in the decade to 2020 as embodied in the LG scenario estimates. In non-OECD economies, underlying growth potentials are significantly higher than in the OECD area, and sound policies should provide an additional growth impulse. The growth dividend associated with good policy would be around 2.5 percentage points over the next 25 years, with GDP growth averaging 6.7 per cent per annum in the HG scenario. In the LG scenario, the growth performance of non-OECD economies would not improve upon the past 25 years.

OECD *economies*

In the OECD area the package of reforms associated with HG would pay off largely in terms of higher productivity growth (see Figure 2.2), counterbalancing the strong negative growth impact of ageing. Moreover, with labour force growing more slowly, and assuming more flexible labour markets, the earlier trend of rising unemployment would be reversed.

Table 2.1 illustrates the effects that demographic changes in major OECD areas may have on their growth rates over the period to 2020. The largest negative impact could be expected in Japan where the average annual GDP growth rate could be reduced by as much as 0.6 per cent per annum. Cumulatively, this would result in a 2020 GDP level 14 per cent lower than with a constant age pyramid. Europe, and to a lesser extent the United States, will also be affected by ageing, with their respective 2020 GDP levels 4.5 per cent and 2.4 per cent lower than with an unchanged population age structure. The effects operate through three main channels: a shrinking labour force, reduced private savings, and increased net government debt and taxes to finance higher government expenditures on pensions and health care. Adverse growth effects could be expected to extend well beyond 2020.

The employment contribution to GDP growth is set to fall steadily over the projection period as slower population growth and population ageing progressively slow the growth of the labour force. In Japan, where the ageing process is advancing most rapidly, the contribution of employment growth to GDP growth would turn negative after 2000. For the European Union, the contribution of employment growth is expected to be negligible under the LG scenario but somewhat greater under the HG scenario due to an assumed reduction in

Box 2.1. Basic Assumptions of the High-Growth (HG) and Low-Growth (LG) Scenarios

	HG	LG
Policy assumptions		
• Trade barriers	Tariff-equivalents fall to zero by 2020	Tariff-equivalents reduced to 50 per cent of their 1992 level
• Export taxes/subsidies	Decline to zero by 2020	Decline to 50 per cent of 1992 level
• Fiscal consolidation	Achievement of targets	No achievement of targets
• Labour-market related reforms	Implementation of the OECD Jobs Strategy	No major improvements with respect to labour-market flexibility
"Technical" assumptions		
• Population growth	Same assumptions as embodied in the latest revision of the UN "medium variant" projections dating from 1996 (see Annex to this chapter)	
• Energy efficiency	Increase of 1 per cent per annum in OECD countries and 2 per cent per annum elsewhere	Increase of 0.8 per cent per annum in OECD countries and 1.5 per cent per annum elsewhere
• World oil prices	Increase of 2 per cent per annum in real terms between 1995 and 2010 and 1 per cent per annum between 2010 and 2020	Increase of 1.5 per cent per annum between 1995 and 2010 and 0.8 per cent per annum between 2010 and 2020
• Crude oil and natural gas extraction rates	No differences between the two scenarios	
• Decline in trade and transport margins	Decrease of 1 per cent per annum	Decrease of 0.8 per cent per annum

Source: OECD Development Centre, 1997.

◆ Figure 2.1. *GDP growth rates*
(percentage rates of increase)

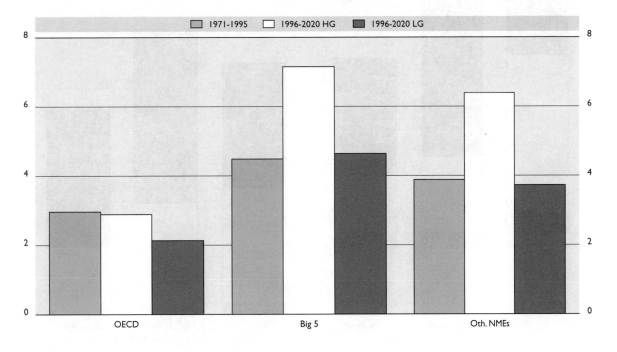

◆ Figure 2.2. ***GDP growth rates and their determinants: OECD economies under high and low growth scenarios***
(percentage points of GDP growth)

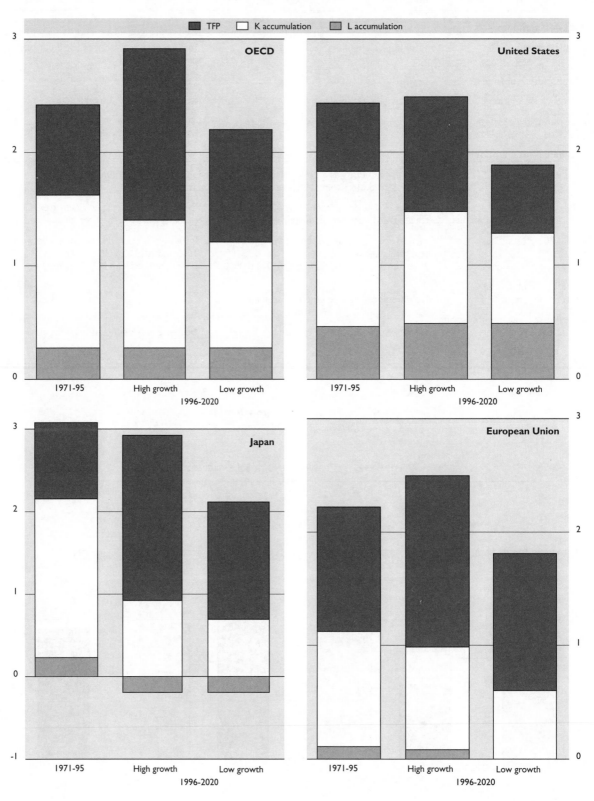

Source: OECD estimates.

Table 2.1. **Effects of demographic changes in major OECD areas to 2020**

Changes in:	Japan			Europe			United States		
	2000	2010	2020	2000	2010	2020	2000	2010	2020
Dependency ratio (% point)	2.8	12.2	21.5	0.4	1.0	5.9	−1.1	−3.6	3.0
GDP growth (% p.a.)	−0.5	−0.8	−0.4	−0.1	−0.1	−0.5	0.2	0.0	−0.6
Investment (% of GDP)	−1.1	−1.9	−1.8	−0.5	−0.5	−1.5	0.0	−0.1	−1.5
Net gov't debt (% of GDP)	0.1	7.8	34.6	0.1	1.5	8.1	0.0	0.4	6.9

Note: The simulations show changes in rates and ratios arising from projected demographic changes to 2020 relative to the assumption of a constant 1995 age pyramid.
Source: OECD simulations.

structural unemployment. By the second decade of the 21st century, the labour force in Europe is projected to begin to shrink and labour force growth in the United States and the rest of the OECD to slow significantly.

What contribution, if any, could international migration make to alleviating the problems of population ageing and slow labour force growth in OECD countries? Modelling work shows that unless net migrant flows were to increase to 5 to 10 times current levels in certain OECD countries, migration could not neutralise the projected rise in old-age dependency ratios and associated fiscal burdens. Continued flows at recent historical rates would have little impact. Projections of international migration flows are extremely hard to make, and the population projections underlying Table 2.1 incorporate a technical assumption about net future migration based on past trends.

The contribution of capital accumulation to GDP growth could be expected to diminish in the future, as savings and investment rates decline. In Japan, investment is projected to fall as a share of GDP by almost 2 percentage points in 2010 from current levels. In the European Union and the United States, the major declines in investment are projected to occur later, reaching 1.5 percentage points of GDP by 2020. Simulations suggest that the effect of fiscal consolidation in offsetting the growth impact of ageing – notably through lower interest rates and higher investment – is modest, except in the United States.

For the OECD as a whole, productivity growth is expected to be the main determinant of long-term output growth, though its contribution may be somewhat smaller in the United States than in Japan or OECD Europe. Four main factors could boost TFP growth under a high growth (HG) scenario: regulatory and other competition-enhancing reforms; faster globalisation and technological progress; and the upgrading of human capital. As noted earlier, Europe and Japan could reap especially large growth dividends from regulatory reforms, since the process is still at a relatively early stage. Globalisation should benefit all OECD regions through gains from greater specialisation and trade as well as through a more efficient global allocation of capital. Information and communication technologies and the organisational changes they induce should raise economy-wide productivity. Besides these technologies, others with sizeable long-run economic potential include biotechnology (in agriculture, health care and environmental remediation), advanced materials (in aerospace, automobiles, electronics, textiles and construction), and alternative energy sources, for example, hydrogen fuel cells for transport and combined cycle gas turbine technology for heating and electricity generation. A highly educated workforce will be required to take full advantage of many of these new technologies. In combination, these factors could yield TFP growth over the scenario period equal to or slightly higher than the rates of the 1970s.

High future growth in the non-OECD economies can be expected to result from the interaction of a combination of factors: expansion and upgrading of the quality of the labour force, high rates of savings and capital accumulation, inter-sectoral resource transfers and strong productivity performance.

Labour force expansion, including a growing share of formal sector employment, will be a modest contributor to economic growth in the non-OECD economies during the next 25 years. Its importance will gradually diminish as a consequence of declining birth rates and longer formal education in an increasing number of developing economies, and the onset of population ageing in some countries, notably the DAEs, Russia, and China. In Sub-Saharan Africa (SSA), however, the contribution of labour force growth would remain very large, almost one-fourth of GDP growth under the HG scenario assumptions.

High rates of investment in human and physical capital and fast TFP growth are encouraged by sound macroeconomic management and continued institutional and policy reform to foster market competition and more efficient resource allocation. As shown in Figure 2.3, in the high-growth scenario, TFP growth and capital accumulation would contribute almost equally to GDP growth. Even though its relative contribution to GDP growth declines steeply compared to the preceding 25 years, capital accumulation will continue to have a large weight due to high savings and investment rates over the scenario period. Both capital accumulation and TFP might slow somewhat after 2010, as the initial growth impetus from further opening-up of markets and from, financial liberalisation and fiscal consolidation gradually peters out.

In the event of major progress with reform and upgrading of human capital in non-OECD countries, TFP could improve further on the performance of the early 1990s, perhaps even growing at a rate approaching the 3 per cent enjoyed by the dynamic Asian economies during that period. Over time the contribution of capital accumulation to growth should diminish while that of productivity gains should increase. For this to happen, however, larger investments in education and training would be needed to raise the share of skilled labour in the total labour force; this could add as much as one percentage point to GDP growth rates in non-OECD economies. For the countries of the Middle East and North Africa and of Sub-Saharan Africa where TFP growth was negative through the 1980s and early 1990s. Thus, even moderately positive TFP growth, sustained over a 25-year period, would represent an important turnaround.

Following a decade of extraordinarily rapid but unbalanced economic growth, with intermittent high inflation, in a high-growth scenario China would experience somewhat lower growth rates (see Figure 2.4). Given China's already low population growth, per capita GDP could grow at a rate close to that enjoyed by the DAEs in the 1970s and 1980s. The gains expected from further liberalisation and domestic deregulation could be very significant for highly-regulated economies like India's. Thus, over the next 25 years, under a high-growth scenario, India's growth rate would exceed by a wide margin the rate of the last quarter century. Although it would not likely achieve a growth explosion comparable to that of China after the opening up in 1979, India could progressively close the growth gap with its giant neighbour, becoming a dynamic pole of attraction for foreign investment. Emerging from the severe recession of the early 1990s, Russia and other Republics of the NIS will likely record moderate growth to 2000, after which growth would accelerate. Even in the HG scenario, however, it may take as long as ten years for the Russian economy to get back to the pre-transition GDP level (compared to 15 years in the LG scenario). Brazil and Indonesia would also enjoy high growth, with the former improving on and the latter sustaining its recent growth performance, attributable in considerable measure to a significant boost in TFP growth.

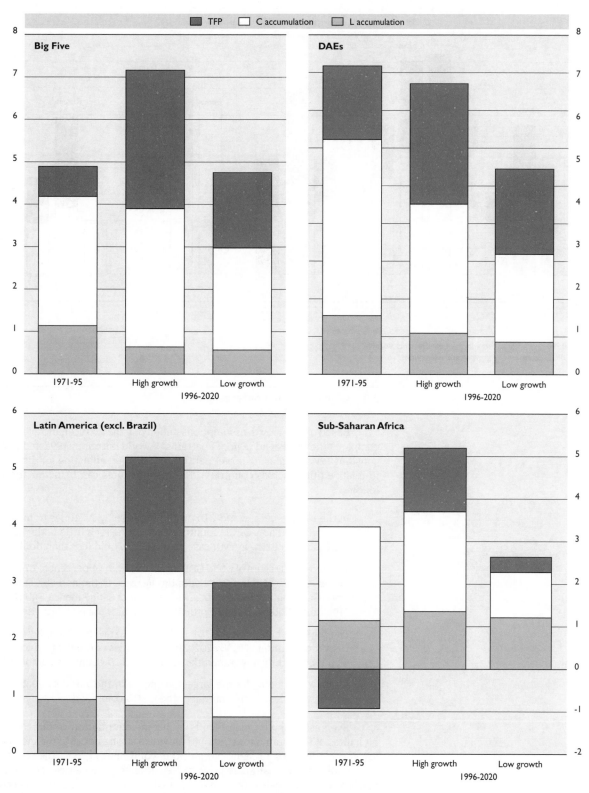

◆ Figure 2.3. **GDP growth rates: non-OECD economies**
(percentage points of GDP growth)

Source: OECD estimates.

◆ Figure 2.4. **Contribution to GDP growth for the Big Five, 1971-1995 and 1996-2020**
(percentage points of GDP growth)

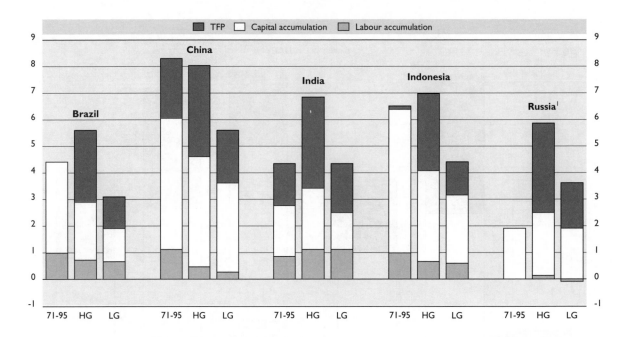

1. 1971-1990 only, with no breakdown of determinants available.
Source: OECD estimates and growth rate assumptions.

2.2. Global Income Convergence

Based on the growth assumptions underlying the two scenarios, Figure 2.5 compares the levels and regional patterns of world output in 1995 and 2020 at constant 1992 purchasing power parities, or PPPs (*i.e.* adjusting for differences in relative prices across countries). The main features can be summarised as follows:

– In the HG scenario, world GDP would increase by 2.5 times from 1995 to 2020, with the non-OECD countries accounting for a little under half that increase. In the low growth case, world GDP would less than double.

– The non-OECD share of world GDP would rise from 44 per cent to 67 per cent (56 per cent in LG). In LG, most of the increase in the non-OECD share of world GDP would reflect growth in Asia; shares for Latin America, Sub-Saharan Africa and Middle East and North Africa would stagnate or decrease.

– The Big Five share of world GDP is projected to rise from roughly one-fifth to over one-third in HG. By 2020, the economies of the Big Five combined would be slightly larger than those of the OECD countries combined.

– China would be by far the largest economy in the world by 2020, with a GDP slightly less than half that of the OECD combined.

Even assuming no major shifts in income distribution within countries, high rates of long-term growth should provide a strong boost to the incomes of low-income families in many parts of the world, making possible significant further inroads into hard-core poverty. Nevertheless, even a quarter century of high growth would leave the average per capita income of non-OECD economies far below the OECD average and Sub-Saharan Africa would hardly see a

◆ Figure 2.5. ***Shares in world GDP, 1995 and 2020***
(in 92 US$, using PPP exchange rates)

1995: 32 trillion

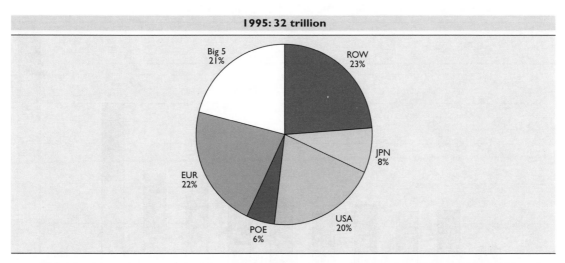

2020 HG: 106 trillion

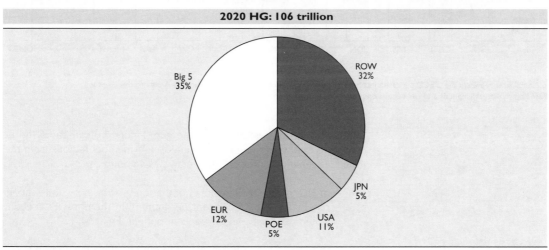

2020 LG: 70 trillion

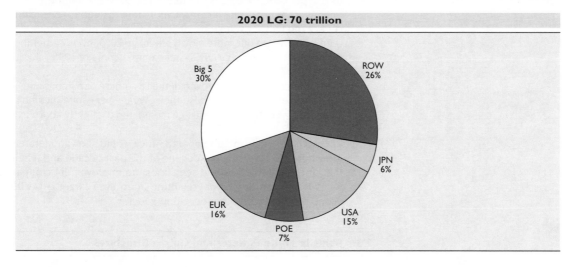

Note: See Annex to this Chapter for the definition of country groupings.
Source: Calculated from growth assumptions for HG and LG scenarios.

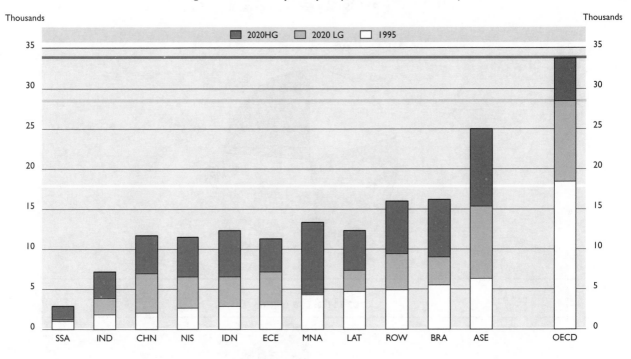

Thousands

2020HG   2020 LG   1995

Thousands

Note: Horizontal lines represent the OECD per capita income average. For definition of country groupings, see Annex to this chapter.
Source: Based on growth assumptions and UN population projections underlying the scenarios.

narrowing of its per capita income gap. Figure 2.6 compares the per capita incomes that would result in the major non-member regions from the HG and the LG scenarios to the OECD average. Main points are:

– In HG, given OECD's slow population growth, per capita income would rise by almost 2.5 per cent per annum; in the non-OECD economies, it would rise an average 5 per cent per annum.

– In HG, per capita incomes would tend to converge. In non-OECD economies average per capita income would more than double, reaching 32 per cent of the OECD average by 2020. In LG, per capita incomes would still tend to converge but more slowly; thus, by 2020, no non-member region would reach the average OECD per capita income of 1995.

– In HG, the continued fast growth of the Dynamic Asian Economies (roughly "ASE" in the Figure) would raise their average per capita income to within three-fourths of the OECD average (compared to slightly above half in LG).

– Per capita incomes in Sub-Saharan Africa would show moderately strong growth in HG, reversing the decline of the past decade and a half. In LG, the African continent would see almost no improvement compared with its 1995 per capita income, resulting in an even larger gap with OECD economies and with other developing regions.

2.3. Shifts in Trade Patterns and Output Structures

Liberalisation of trade as well as falling transport and communication costs – features of the HG scenario – would work together to boost

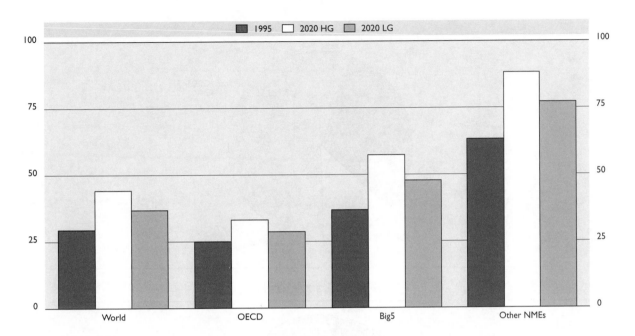

◆ Figure 2.7. **Trade to GDP ratios in 1995 and 2020**
(in per cent)

Note: For data reasons, the trade figures used in the model exclude most intra-regional trade.
Source: OECD LINKAGE model.

international commerce. (Note that the absolute size of regional current account balances to 2020 is assumed to remain constant in both scenarios.) In the HG case, trade would increase over the scenario period more rapidly than world output, growing three-and-a-half times in value terms and rising from 30 per cent of world GDP in 1995 to about 45 per cent in 2020 (see Figure 2.7). OECD trade would expand somewhat more slowly than non-OECD economies' trade, partly because Members' trade barriers are already low in the base year and so the removal of tariffs would provide less of a stimulus. By contrast, in the non-OECD economies the removal of relatively high import tariffs, particularly in India, China and Brazil, would raise significantly their exposure to trade. On average, among the Big Five, the ratio of trade to GDP would rise by more than half.

These trends are reflected in the changes in regional trade patterns (see Figure 2.8):

– In HG, most striking would be the steep decline of the intra-OECD share in world trade (from just under one-half to less than a third) and the parallel rise in intra-NME trade (from a tenth to more than a fifth). In LG, these two changes in regional trade patterns would also occur but would be less pronounced.

– In the HG scenario, almost half of the increase in world trade over the period would consist of trade between OECD countries and the non-OECD economies, and only one-fifth of that increase would consist of intra-OECD trade. In 2020, trade with the Big Five would account for about one-fifth of total OECD trade and trade with other non-OECD countries for just over 40 per cent.

◆ Figure 2.8. **Regional patterns of trade**
(total trade in 92 US$)

1995: 3.835 billion

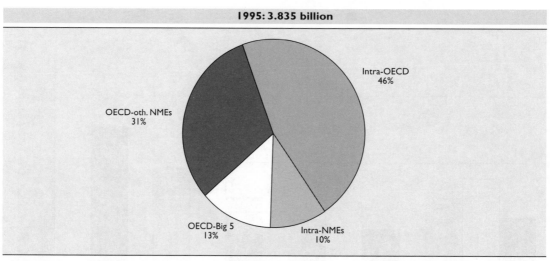

Intra-OECD
46%

OECD-oth. NMEs
31%

OECD-Big 5
13%

Intra-NMEs
10%

2020 HG: 13.221 billion

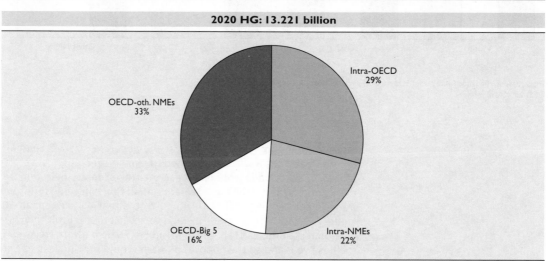

Intra-OECD
29%

OECD-oth. NMEs
33%

OECD-Big 5
16%

Intra-NMEs
22%

2020 LG: 8.655 billion

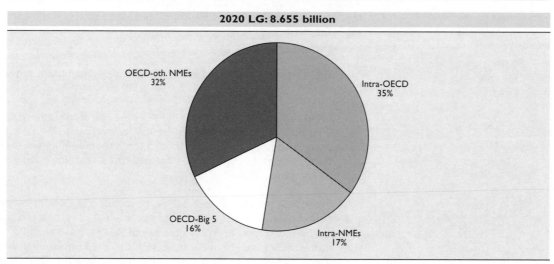

OECD-oth. NMEs
32%

Intra-OECD
35%

OECD-Big 5
16%

Intra-NMEs
17%

Source: OECD LINKAGE Model.

Under the HG scenario, world exports would increase almost three-and-a-half times between 1995 and 2020. Consumer goods exports, led by textiles and apparel, would rise particularly rapidly as would agricultural and food products, in large part due to the elimination of high trade barriers (see Figure 2.9). World exports of capital goods – consisting of, among others, transport equipment, electrical and non-electrical machinery – would grow at only a slightly slower pace. Services trade is very likely to have been underestimated since the database used for the model simulations does not incorporate the high barriers to such trade in the base year, so benefits from liberalisation are not captured.

With the removal of tariffs on skill-intensive capital goods and given the high rates of investment in non-OECD economies, OECD capital goods exports to those countries would increase almost fivefold. Among the OECD countries, Japan would specialise the most heavily on producing and exporting capital goods, with its capital goods exports benefiting from strong growth anticipated in Asian markets. Consumer goods exporters in non-OECD economies would benefit from fast-growing imports into OECD countries as well as growing "South-South" trade. Among the Big Five, China would post the most impressive export performance, with the share of its exports in the world total doubling to just under 13 per cent by 2020. China would overtake Europe to become the largest consumer goods exporter, while the other East Asian economies would also post strong consumer goods export growth. Beyond the Big Five and the East Asian economies, most other non-OECD economies would remain rather small exporters of manufactures.

Another indicator of the growing importance of international trade to national economies is the degree of import penetration, measured as the share of imports in domestic consumption. In the OECD area, agricultural and consumer goods would be the most affected by changes in the degree of import penetration (see Figure 2.10), as these sectors enjoyed heavy protection at the start of the scenario period. Thus, in these two sectors more than elsewhere, further adjustment would be needed in coming years. The scope for adjustment existing in non-OECD countries in an era of global free trade is significantly bigger. Import penetration would also rise substantially in these two output areas in the Big Five and the rest of the non-OECD economies. Removal of trade barriers will affect their heavily-protected sectors just as it will those in the Member countries, and these sectors represent a larger share of their GDP than the few ones in the OECD area still subject to high rates of protection. Import penetration in the capital goods sector would rise less significantly in the Big Five and in other non-OECD economies since their domestic industries would also grow rapidly. In terms of import volumes, however, non-OECD economies would represent about 45 per cent of total capital goods imports in 2020.

Viewed against declining world market shares, increasing import penetration of domestic markets by non-OECD economies, strengthening of competition (notably from East Asia) for an increasing range of capital goods, future international trade prospects would, at first glance, not seem particularly promising for OECD economies. What are the opportunities stemming from international trade that would make these future challenges and adjustments not only supportable for OECD societies but even beneficial, convincing them to embark on a fast globalisation track? Three arguments make the case for globalisation powerfully.

First, the removal of trade barriers to food products and consumer goods would reduce their end-use prices in OECD countries. Morever, when compared with OECD manufactured export prices, the international prices of these imports

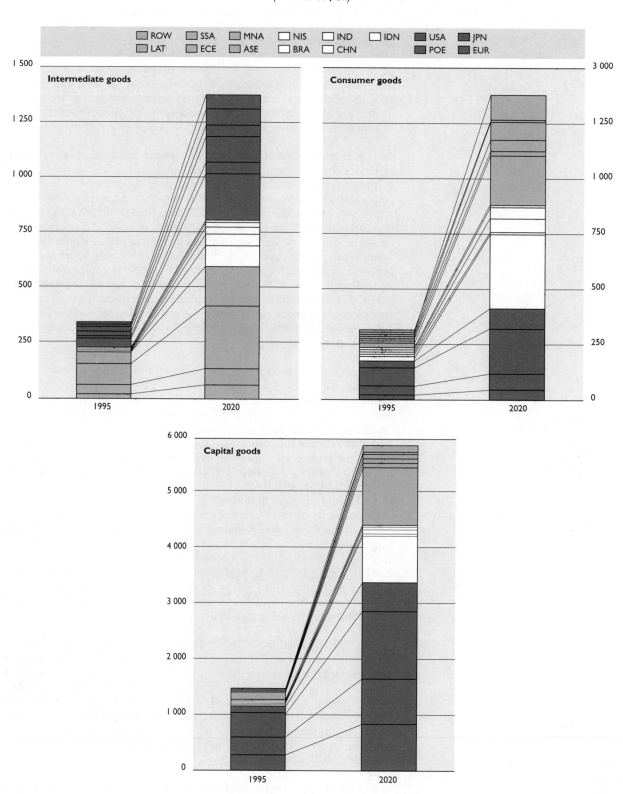

◆ Figure 2.9. **Manufactures export structure by region, 1995-2020**
(in 1992 US$ bn)

Source: OECD Linkage Model.

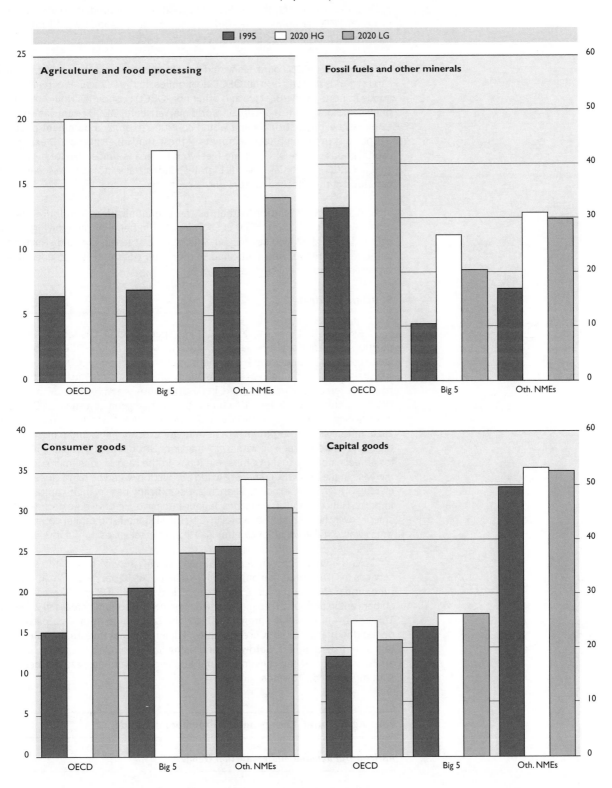

◆ Figure 2.10. **Degree of import penetration, 1995 and 2020**
(in per cent)

■ 1995 □ 2020 HG ▨ 2020 LG

Agriculture and food processing

OECD   Big 5   Oth. NMEs

Fossil fuels and other minerals

OECD   Big 5   Oth. NMEs

Consumer goods

OECD   Big 5   Oth. NMEs

Capital goods

OECD   Big 5   Oth. NMEs

Note: Import penetration is defined as imports as a share of apparent consumption (*i.e.* production minus exports plus imports).
Source: OECD LINKAGE model.

would fall rather significantly (for example, the relative price of textile and apparel goods could decline by some 40 per cent over the scenario period). As OECD economies increasingly import low-tech goods that are produced more cheaply in non-OECD economies, the fall in price of those goods would raise real purchasing power of OECD consumers.

Second, OECD countries would benefit strongly from the rapid growth of capital goods imports by non-OECD economies. In the HG scenario, real capital goods imports by the Big Five and other non-OECD economies would be multiplied six-fold. Despite a decline in world market share, OECD countries' exports would still expand strongly and would continue to enjoy a dominant position – especially in the high-tech segments of these markets. Thus, OECD exports of capital goods to non-OECD economies would increase almost five-fold. A further shift in OECD economies towards high-tech industrial sectors would secure high paid jobs in the exposed sectors of the economy.

A third consideration is that, as the communications revolution makes more services tradeable, OECD economies should benefit from growing export demand for high-skilled services, in which some at least enjoy a distinct comparative advantage. As mentioned earlier, this potential is not adequately captured by the model simulations.

Structure of output

As a result of increasing international specialisation, changes in the composition of output could be large in OECD as well as in non-OECD economies (see Figure 2.11). Under the HG scenario, the share of non-OECD economies in sectoral output would increase across the board. The sectors most affected by a complete removal of trade barriers in OECD countries and faster growth in non-OECD economies would be agriculture and consumer goods. The non-OECD share of world agricultural production would grow significantly to more than half in 2020. In this sector, output growth in non-OECD economies, and particularly in the Big Five, would keep up with a growing domestic demand. The same is true of fossil fuels, notably coal in China and India. In the case of consumer goods, the increase in the non-OECD share of world production would be more closely associated with growing exports, financing a significant rise in their capital goods imports. Hence, in OECD countries, labour-intensive sectors would decline rather steeply over the scenario period relative to the skill-intensive capital goods sector, which would still account for two-thirds of world capital goods output in 2020.

As the OECD economies are already heavily service-based, the share of services in GDP would rise only slightly, to just over 70 per cent in 2020. By that time, under the HG scenario, the share of services in GDP would reach about 60 per cent in non-OECD economies, a five percentage point increase in 25 years. This relatively moderate growth reflects the commodity-intensive pattern of demand in many non-OECD economies. High industrial investment rates sustain strong demand for "hardware" and rising household incomes from low levels boost demand for consumer durables before spending patterns begin to shift more heavily towards services.

2.4. Agricultural, Energy and Environmental Trends

Agricultural demand and production trends

Concerns have been raised regarding the capacity of agricultural supply to keep pace with anticipated growth in demand, notably in the large, rapidly growing Asian economies. Growth in demand for agricultural goods

◆ Figure 2.11. *Regional composition of world output by sector, HG*

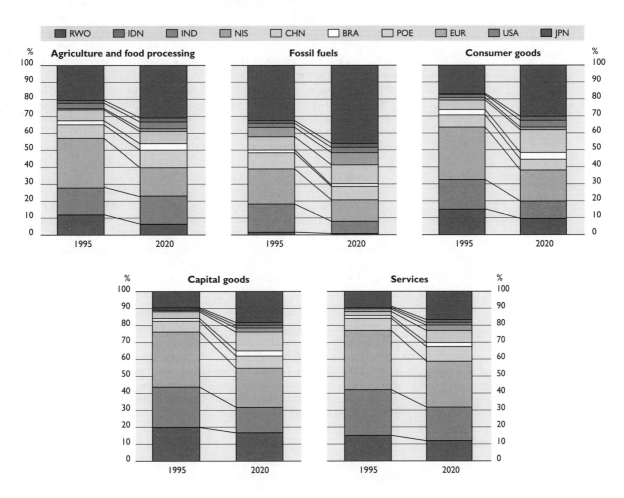

Source: OECD LINKAGE model.

over the quarter century ending in 2020 is expected to be close to that experienced over the preceding one. While under the HG scenario world GDP growth would be faster than in the past, income elasticities of demand for food will tend to fall with rising income and wealth; at the same time, world population growth will be considerably slower. In view of these trends, agricultural demand patterns could be expected to shift towards high-value food products and non-food products (*e.g.*, fibres, hides and skins, tobacco, etc.). The growth in world demand for food would occur largely in non-OECD economies (some 80 per cent of incremental demand), a consequence of their faster population growth and their strong income growth from relatively low levels.

Expecting reasonably strong productivity growth to be sustainable, no global food crisis seems likely to occur during the projection period. In a HG scenario, the global agricultural output growth rate, needed to satisfy the expected growth in world demand to 2020, would be 2.5 per cent per annum, almost identical with an FAO estimate for the period 1972-1992. Past growth has been accompanied by a downward trend in international commodity prices for foodstuffs and other agricultural produce relative to the price of manufactures. Given the highly competitive, export-oriented agricultures of

North America and Australia, this trend may well persist. Indeed, the farming systems of Canada, the United States and Australia benefit from a favourable endowment of land and a well-developed research capacity, which, together with an efficient agricultural services industry, should ensure the continued generation of higher crop yields and outputs at low cost. The technological dynamism of these farming industries (coupled with strong growth in output elsewhere, notably in Latin America) could thus continue to tilt commodity prices against agriculture over the longer term, though this is obviously sensitive to the fortunes of agriculture in the big consuming countries. Thus, if agricultural productivity were to increase by only 1 per cent per annum (rather than 1.5 per cent assumed under HG), world agricultural prices would not change with respect to the price of other goods.

Although world trade in agricultural products will expand rapidly, the growing food needs of large countries and regions are likely to be met mainly locally. In general, under falling relative prices, agricultural output can keep growing where there is cheap new land to develop (more irrigation would serve the same purpose) or as a result of favourable developments in cost-reducing technologies. A third possibility – but one increasingly disfavoured – would be (increasing) subsidies to farmers, which make crops profitable for them to grow although unprofitable at market prices.

Of these possibilities to keep up production growth, technological advance has been by far the most important one in recent years. This is bound to remain so in the future: there is little new land to develop in the world as a whole (and what there is, is not at low cost) and farm subsidies would decline as part of the move to do away with trade barriers in agriculture. It follows that cost-reducing innovation must be generated in or be applicable to a broad range of major countries and regions if the growth and price projections for agricultural products, embodied in the HG and the LG scenarios, are to be validated.

Changes in trade barriers condition the supply response of agriculture in the main producing areas. The major impacts likely will concern the OECD countries themselves, where the low cost producers of North America, Australia and Latin America would supply a larger share of the demands of European and to a lesser extent Japanese consumers (see Figure 2.12). Among the non-OECD economies, the impact of trade barriers is much more variable, since in some cases protection has been to the advantage of consumers not producers, as governments have sought to keep prices low. In 2020, the major non-member country importers would be in Asia, notably East Asia and China, and in the Middle East/North Africa region.

The Big Five would account for over 40 per cent of the incremental demand for agricultural commodities, due mostly to higher demand in China and India. While in 2020 China's agricultural and processed food imports would account for roughly one-third of the non-member country total, they would represent only 15 per cent of the world total. Still, if – as the HG scenario implicitly assumes – China were to forsake food self-sufficiency as a policy goal, it could emerge as a sizeable net agricultural importer by 2020 (Figure 2.12), on a par with Japan. China's self-sufficiency ratio would decline, with agriculture and food processing imports rising to one-third of domestic consumption by 2020. A very sizeable share of those imports would consist of animal feeds and of livestock to satisfy consumers' growing taste for meat and dairy products. Indeed, the much higher projected future per capita meat consumption in China than in India is a major factor explaining the former's growing agricultural imports and the latter's continued self-sufficiency (indeed, slightly positive agricultural trade balance in 2020).

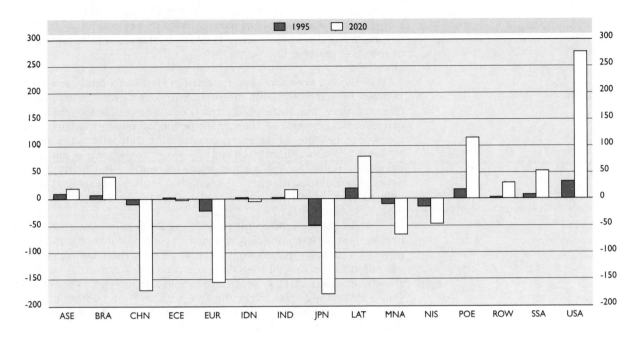

◆ Figure 2.12. **Net trade in agriculture and food processing**
(constant 1992 US$ billions)

Source: OECD LINKAGE model.

Energy market trends

Under the HG scenario, world energy demand would grow at 3.1 per cent per annum, somewhat slower than the growth in world GDP, reflecting an assumed improvement in energy efficiency in both OECD and non-OECD countries. The LG scenario is associated with marginally smaller energy efficiency gains but with significantly slower growth in energy demand (2.1 per cent per annum).

Factors bearing on the future level and pattern of energy demand include: *a*) a likely increase in the non-member economy share of world production of energy-intensive industries, *b*) the relatively low energy efficiencies (high use of energy per unit of output) in those countries due to less than state-of-the-art technology and, frequently, inefficient energy pricing policies, and *c*) the ongoing and probably accelerating switch from non-commercial sources of energy (like fuelwood and agricultural wastes) to commercial ones. The share of the non-OECD economies in world demand for fossil fuels is estimated under the HG scenario at some two-thirds of the total in 2020 compared with roughly half in 1995.

At the world level, existing energy resources are thought to be sufficient to meet rising energy demand. Nevertheless, for the non-OECD economies in particular, the investment requirements for fossil fuel extraction, transportation, electricity generation, etc., will have high opportunity costs viewed either as a sacrifice of investment capital that might otherwise be used elsewhere in the economy or in terms of foregone consumption. Particularly in China and India, a large part of the energy investment will be related to the extraction, transportation and consumption of coal, even though coal requires costly and relatively complex technology to burn efficiently and cleanly.

Under the impetus of rapidly growing demand, the East Asia region (including China, Indonesia and Japan) could become the largest region in terms of net oil imports, with dependence on oil rising from two-thirds at present to almost 90 per cent by 2020. The Middle East's dominance of fossil fuels trade would increase markedly, with its net exports in 2020 some two-and-a-half times those of the NIS, the only other major fossil fuel exporter by then (see Figure 2.13).

In the HG scenario, world electricity demand would grow by half between 1995 and 2020, with the non-OECD countries accounting for over three-fourths of that increase. Electricity would be the fastest growing form of final energy demand over the scenario period, continuing a long-term trend increase of its share in final energy consumption. This reflects the tendency for substitution away from fossil fuel end-use, the emergence of new ways of using electricity through technological innovation and, particularly in developing countries, the expansion of the distribution network and the wider diffusion of electrical appliances.

While the fuel choice for power generation may change somewhat from current patterns (industry restructuring, deregulation and increasing private sector participation would all play a part in this), the big shift into gas noted in the case of the OECD could probably not occur so rapidly elsewhere because of lack of access to supplies. Hydroelectric power would show substantial growth in the Big Five, with the Three Gorges project in China and Narmada in India major contributors to that growth; hydro capacity could more than double by 2010, though at some point the pace of expansion might well be slowed by the absence of new low-cost sites,

◆ Figure 2.13. **Net trade in fossil fuels, HG**
(constant 1992 US$ billions)

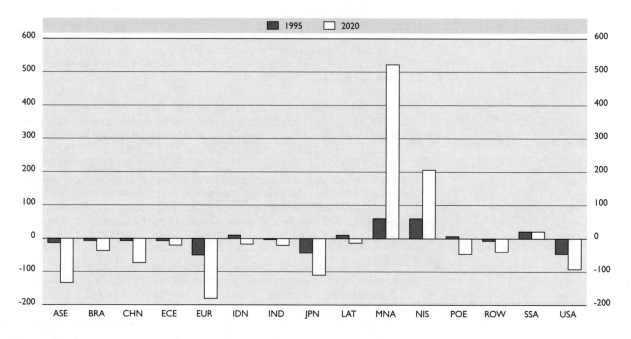

Source: OECD LINKAGE model.

social concerns (the resettlement necessitated by the creation of large reservoirs) and for environmental reasons. Finally, some countries have a nuclear power generation investment programme but investments in new nuclear power plants have slowed down greatly and the future of nuclear power deployment will depend on the capacity to maintain its economic competitivity in the long term.

Fast-growing demands for energy will require a combination of supply responses, largely from coal, oil and gas, plus some additional electricity generated by hydro and nuclear power. If there are no major technological breakthroughs or new measures to restrict CO_2 emissions, none of the non-traditional renewable sources of energy, such as wind and solar, seems likely to make much impact: the IEA projects their collective contribution in 2010 at less than one per cent of the total. However, even without taking into account the uncertainty regarding the future stance of environmental policies, such projections contain wide margins of uncertainty after 2010, reflecting the unpredictability of technology development and its impact on output in the long term. If binding international agreements to restrict CO_2 emissions are reached, non-traditional renewables would become more competitive, increasing their market share more rapidly. Such a development would also stimulate research efforts and process innovation, leading to a more rapid decline in the cost of these renewable sources of energy.

Global environmental trends

A pressing environmental concern associated with the expected rise in fossil-fuel-based energy consumption over the scenario period is the projected rise in global emissions of carbon dioxide (CO_2) and other greenhouse gases (GHG) that contribute to global warming. Thus far, progress has been slow in OECD countries towards controlling CO_2 emissions, despite the commitments made under the Framework Convention on Climate Change (see Box 2.3). In the absence of new initiatives, the increase in atmospheric CO_2 concentration is set to be very large in the next 25 years. Given the expected future contributions of non-OECD countries to GHG emissions, any solution to the problem will have to involve their co-operation.

Fossil fuel production and use represent about three-quarters of man-made CO_2 emissions, and fossil fuels still account for 85-90 per cent of commercial energy

Box 2.3. Global Climate Change

Signatories to the Framework Convention on Climate Change (FCCC) have set themselves the goal of stabilising greenhouse gas (GHG) concentrations in the atmosphere at a level that would prevent dangerous anthropogenic interference with the climate system (FCCC, Article 2). OECD and other industrialised countries have an obligation under the Convention to provide leadership in the international effort to achieve this objective. Industrialised (Annex 1) countries are committed as a group to adopt national policies and programmes aiming to stabilise GHG emissions at 1990 levels by the year 2000. OECD governments have made some progress in establishing policy frameworks for GHG reduction, but most are having trouble achieving short-term targets. Recent indicators show that many OECD countries will not achieve their national targets for GHG reductions in 2000. Moreover, they are not likely to achieve deep reductions in GHG emissions over the longer term without a major new commitment to action.

The Intergovernmental Panel on Climate Change (IPCC) estimates that global mean temperature has increased between 0.3 and 0.6 °C and the global sea level has risen an average of 1.0 to 2.5 millimetres per year over the past century, concluding in its 1995 scientific assessment that there has been a "discernible human influence on climate". Climate models project (based on IPCC emission scenarios) over the next century a climate sensitivity in the range of 1.5 to 4.5 C° (*i.e.* centigrade degrees) and a sea level rise of 15 cm. to 95 cm., with 2.5 C° and 50 cm. as the central best estimates. In all cases the average rate of warming would probably be greater than any seen in the past 10 000 years. Even if global carbon emissions were to be stabilised at 1990 levels, atmospheric CO_2 concentrations would go on rising for at least another century, reaching 500 ppmv by 2100 (compared to a current level of 360 ppmv). Climate-induced environmental changes cannot be reversed quickly, if at all, due to the long time scales associated with the climate system. Decisions taken during the next few years may limit the range of possible policy options in the future because high near-term emissions would require deeper reductions in the future to meet any given target concentration. Delaying action might reduce overall costs of mitigation because of potential technological advances but also risks increasing the rate, the eventual magnitude, and the global impact of climate change.

Studies of the potential damage costs from climate change show wide variation in the range of costs, stemming in large part from differences in methodology and assumptions. None of the studies can take account of some of the more extreme possible impacts, in particular the unknown probability of catastrophic effects (*e.g.* those associated with a melting of polar ice caps or the extensive loss of carbon-absorbing northern and temperate boreal forests). Also, most valuation studies tend to underestimate the true costs to society of climate change by failure to capture adequately such difficult-to-value costs as impairment of ecosystem function and biodiversity loss.

There may be significant regional variations in climate change and the associated impacts. Research on agricultural impacts suggests that, while global food production would not necessarily experience large reductions, crop yields at low latitudes (particularly in Africa, South Asia, Central and northern South America) could be rather adversely affected – *e.g.* from shortened growing cycles and greater heat and water stress, even allowing for beneficial CO_2 direct effects on yields. These developing regions tend still to depend heavily on their agricultural sectors not only for food security but as a source of income. While in theory they could import more food from higher latitude countries enjoying increased production, how they might finance those imports is unclear.

Source: OECD (1995), Global Warming: Economic Dimensions and Policy Responses, Paris; also, World Resources Institute (1996), World Resources: A Guide to the Global Environment, Washington DC; IPCC SAR, "Climate Change 1995. Impacts, Adaptation and Mitigation of Climate Change: Scientific-Technical Analysis" (Working Group II Report); Parry and Rosenzweig (1994),"Potential impact of climate change on world food supply", Nature, Vol. 367.

use in the world. In the HG scenario and in the absence of policy offsets, world fossil fuel consumption would grow by 3 per cent per year, or by well over 100 per cent during the period. Given the close link between fossil fuel consumption and CO_2 emissions, the latter could be expected to rise by a comparable amount. They would grow even faster than world GDP, because of the increasing weight of coal (a carbon-rich fuel) in the global primary energy mix (from 28 to 35 per cent). Coal also tends to be a particularly dirty fuel and thus increased atmospheric loadings of SO_2 and other air pollutants could be expected. Nuclear energy, supplying bulk electricity, can significantly reduce several atmospheric pollutants, including CO_2, as has been demonstrated by the experience of OECD countries, and will therefore remain a valuable source of carbon-free energy, provided reactors continue to be operated safely and technical solutions to waste-disposal are accepted.

Given their relatively high GDP growth and the relatively high energy-intensity and CO_2-intensity of that growth (compared to OECD countries) (see Figure 1.9 in Chapter 1), the non-OECD countries – and in particular the Big Five – will be major contributors to the increase in global CO_2 emissions over the next 25 years and beyond. Under the HG scenario, the Big Five could account for about 43 per cent, and non-OECD countries as a group for over three-fourths, of the increase in global carbon emissions to 2020. If so, the share of the non-OECD area in global CO_2 emissions in 2020 would be two-thirds, up from roughly half at present. China's increase in emissions to 2020 would be greater than the increase of the entire OECD combined, and India's increase would be roughly as large as that of the United States.

Figure 2.14 shows the trajectories of emissions for Annex 1 industrialised countries as well as for other countries under the HG and LG scenarios; also shown is the 1990 emissions level for Annex 1 countries, at which they have agreed to try to stabilise emissions by the year 2000. While collectively the Annex 1 countries would not greatly exceed this level in 2000, this is attributable almost exclusively to the steep drop in emissions from the CEEC and NIS. In either scenario, OECD countries' emissions would continue to rise without further policy action. Simulations suggest that, even with low growth, in order for OECD countries to stabilise CO_2 emissions at 1990 levels by the year 2000 they would need to realise annual energy efficiency improvements in the range of 3 per cent per annum, two percentage points higher than those assumed in the baseline scenario (and in most climate change models). Such gains are highly unlikely with the incentives provided by current energy prices and taxes. By way of comparison, in the decade following the oil price shock of the early 1970s, reductions in the energy intensity of United States GDP averaged slightly under 2 per cent per annum. For the OECD as a whole, energy intensity of GDP fell by an average 1.8 per cent per annum between 1973 and 1988.

The HG scenario results show a significant shift in the location of energy-intensive industries over the scenario period towards the non-OECD economies (see Figure 2.15). This reflects in part at least the relatively cheap energy supplies at their disposal. If structural change were to occur on this scale (with the non-OECD share of global energy-intensive industrial production rising from 21 per cent to 39 per cent), the implications for the global environment could be highly detrimental, unless new energy-intensive industries in the Big Five were at least as energy-efficient as those in the OECD area. At present, this is far from the case. For example, as of 1992-93, the energy intensity of China and India's steel industries (measured as tonnes of oil equivalent per tonne of crude steel) was almost three times that of Japan and Korea. A variety of factors explain this, including the continued heavy reliance on energy-intensive open hearth furnaces, which still account for almost a quarter of Indian steel production (down from over half in 1983) and 15 per cent of Chinese production. The removal of remaining industrial energy subsidies in those countries, combined with greater exposure to international competition, would go some way towards improving energy efficiency levels.

A more positive scenario could materialise if energy efficiency improves rapidly and if non-fossil based energy systems develop more rapidly (hydrogen based fuel cells for cars would be one example). The impact of technological improvements is apt to be greater in rapidly growing economies like China and India than in the OECD countries, because in the former a higher proportion of the energy-using capital stock represents new investment. As noted above, the energy-to-GDP ratio in China has already fallen quite markedly in recent years, albeit from very high levels.

2.5. Global Capital Flows

In the past, the domestic savings of the non-OECD economies and their investments have been closely matched (see Table 2.2). The developing world as a whole (even during the emerging markets boom ahead of Mexico's 1995 crisis) has relied on foreign savings to only a very limited extent: 1.5 per cent in terms of GDP and 6 per cent in terms of investment. Asia has drawn to an even lesser extent on foreign savings for its vibrant growth, just 0.5 per cent of its combined domestic product.

◆ Figure 2.14. ***Carbon emissions, 1990-2020***
(billion tons of carbon)

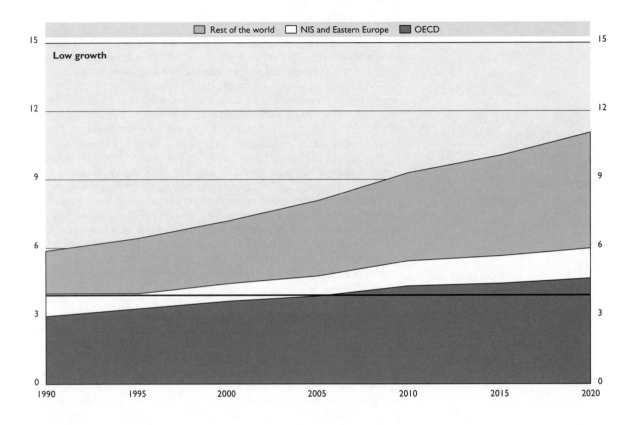

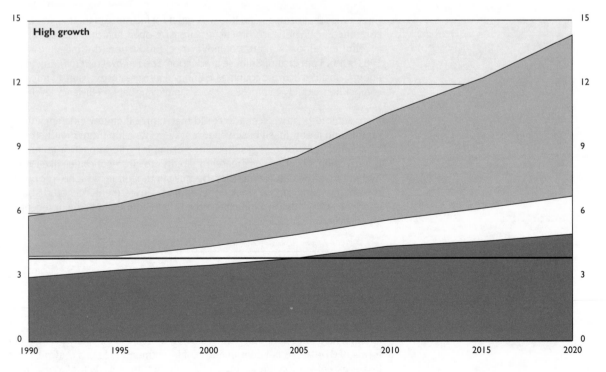

Source: OECD LINKAGE model.

◆ Figure 2.15. ***Regional distribution of energy-intensive industrial output***

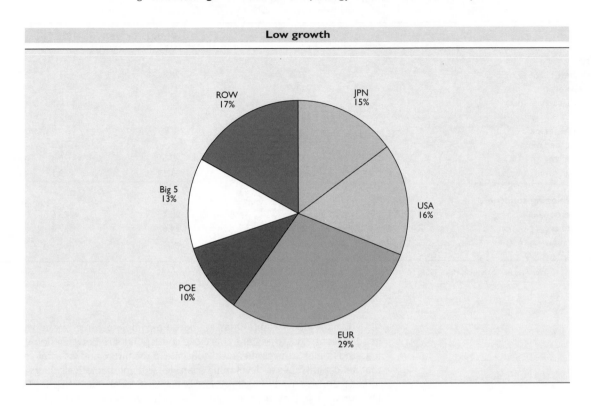

Low growth

ROW
17%

JPN
15%

USA
16%

Big 5
13%

POE
10%

EUR
29%

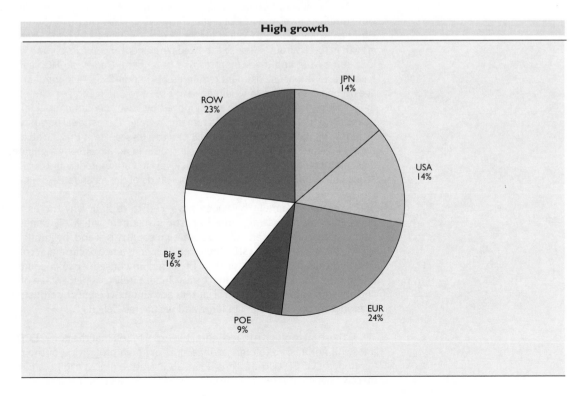

High growth

ROW
23%

JPN
14%

USA
14%

Big 5
16%

POE
9%

EUR
24%

Source: OECD LINKAGE model.

Table 2.2. **Saving and investment in non-member economies**
Percentage of GDP

	1973-80	1981-90	1990-94
Asia			
Domestic savings	25.5	28.1	31.4
Investment	28.6	31.9	
Foreign savings (net)	–0.5	–0.5	–0.5
Latin America			
Domestic savings	20.5	19.4	18.3
Investment	23.8	20.5	20.4
Foreign savings (net)	–3.3	–1.1	–2.1
All developing countries			
Domestic savings	25.7	23.1	25.6
Investment	25.7	24.6	27.2
Foreign savings (net)	0.0	–1.5	–1.6

Source: IMF, *World Economic Outlook*, May 1995.

Even if global capital markets become completely free by the year 2020, good reasons exist to assume this close correspondence between domestic savings and domestic investment will continue in the future and, as a consequence, that net capital flows to developing countries will not dramatically increase. (The model feature of fixed current account balances is consistent with this.) Declining fertility rates and lower young-age dependency in the developing countries will stimulate household savings, just as growth in their labour force through 2020 will stimulate investment. Domestic corporate savings (in the form of retained earnings) will increase to reflect higher returns on invested capital. Higher trend growth in total output will raise expected permanent-income levels and will cause long-run saving and investment to rise in tandem. Under the HG scenario, to meet the additional investment requirements in non-OECD economies, the average domestic savings rate would need to rise by four percentage points of GDP, a modest increase compared to that enjoyed by East Asia during its high growth phase. Regional disparities would remain. Average domestic savings rates would increase significantly in India, the NIS and to a lesser extent Brazil. The other two Big Five countries, China and Indonesia, would maintain already high rates. Savings rates would reach moderately high levels in Latin America and Sub-Saharan Africa but would still be only around two-thirds of the Asian rates.

Another argument has been advanced to explain why the association between domestic savings and domestic investment will likely remain close. Financial markets are sensitive to sovereign country risk and, by implication, to a country's external debt ratio, the level and persistence of current account deficits, and thus its capacity for debt financing. In consequence, a country's net international indebtedness cannot grow indefinitely as a percentage of its GDP and governments tend to control current account movements by adjusting fiscal or monetary policies to avoid large and protracted deficits.

These factors serve to reconfirm the expectation that the non-OECD economies will not absorb foreign savings at a very high proportion of their output, let alone of OECD output. Thus, fears about future global capital shortages or massive net capital outflows from the OECD area seem misplaced.

Even without major increases in net capital flows from OECD to non-OECD countries over the scenario period, there would still be large gains to be realised from further international portfolio diversification. Realising these gains becomes more urgent as population ageing progresses and pension financing problems become more serious. Given the still young populations in the non-OECD countries, Member and non-member age structures are broadly complementary, offering opportunities for mutual gain analogous to those arising from differing factor endowments. Back-of-the-envelope calculations provide a rough indication of the magnitude of these gains. Under the HG scenario, a halving by 2020 of the home asset bias of OECD institutional investors could plausibly be assumed, *i.e.* a partial move towards a portfolio mix reflecting country shares in world stock market capitalisation. (Even assuming the full removal of legal constraints on foreign investment, other factors would maintain some home bias.) An alternative calculation assumes that pension fund managers would seek to maintain the future purchasing power of pension assets. To the extent that pensioners consume non-traded goods (such as health services) rather than traded goods, institutional assets may be biased toward home securities, with fund managers seeking a foreign exposure comparable to the traded-goods proportion of the basket of goods consumed by the typical pensioner. In practice, in countries where pension funds are not constrained by domestic regulation, a fairly good correlation exists between the import-to-GDP ratio and the share of foreign equities held in institutional equity portfolios (see Figure 2.16).

Based on these alternative portfolio diversification strategies, it is estimated that, by the year 2020, a minimum of 8.5 per cent of total OECD pension assets would be invested in the non-OECD area, implying an annual gross transfer – if unhedged – of $20 billion (in 2000) and $35 billion (in 2020) into

◆ Figure 2.16. ***International diversification of equity portofolios held by OECD pension funds***

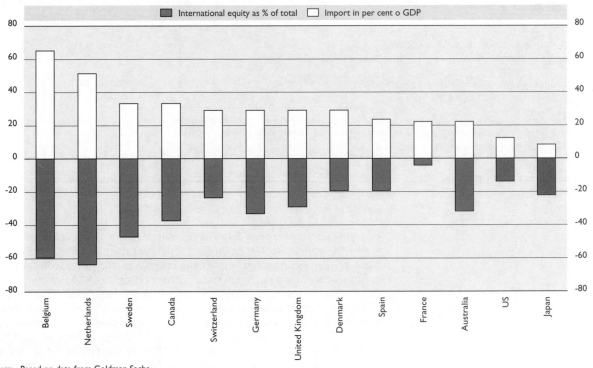

Source: Based on data from Goldman Sachs.

emerging markets (see Box 2.4). The real rate of return of OECD pension assets would rise from 2.8 to 3.0 per cent (a 7.2 per cent rise). Because of the gradual build-up of assets invested in emerging economies, the increase in the rate of return would imply a minimum rise in pension benefits of 2.5 per cent. Among OECD countries, the largest gains would accrue to countries that quickly build a sizeable stock of assets in emerging economies. Nonetheless, even though investing in fast-growing emerging markets would make OECD retirees better off, this would not be enough to finance the additional burden laid on OECD pension systems. Domestic reforms of pensions systems could not be avoided, and key elements of the policy response are likely to include some combination of the following: a shift towards funded pension schemes, closer targeting on poorer retirees, cost containment, and a higher effective retirement age (see next chapter for further discussion).

Under the more conservative of the two sets of assumptions regarding portfolio diversification, non-OECD economies could expect to receive an incremental gross annual portfolio investment amounting to 0.4 per cent of their GDP in 2000 and decreasing to 0.2 per cent in 2020. These portfolio investment flows should be regarded by non-OECD economies as long-term capital inflows given the expected time horizon before major redemption of assets begins to occur. Non-OECD pension funds could also realise diversification gains from investing part of their assets in less volatile OECD stock markets, foregoing some returns for added security.

ANNEX TO CHAPTER 2

Regional Concordance for the LINKAGE Model

1 ASE Other East Asia
Chinese Taipei, Malaysia, Philippines, Singapore, Thailand,

2 BRA Brazil

3 ECE Eastern and Central Europe
Albania, Bulgaria, Czech Republic, Hungary, Poland, Romania, Slovakia, Slovenia

4 CHN China and Hong Kong

5 EUR European Union (15) plus EFTA countries
Austria, Belgium, Denmark, Finland, France, Germany, Greece, Iceland, Ireland, Italy, Luxembourg, Netherlands, Norway, Portugal, Spain, Sweden, Switzerland, United Kingdom

6 IDN Indonesia

7 IND India

8 JPN Japan

9 LAT Rest of Latin America
Antigua and Barbuda, Bahamas, Barbados, Belize, Costa Rica, Cuba, Dominica, Dominican Republic, El Salvador, Grenada, Guatemala, Haiti, Honduras, Jamaica, Nicaragua, Panama, St. Kitts and Nevis, St. Lucia, St. Vincent, Trinidad and Tobago, Argentina, Chile, Bolivia, Colombia, Ecuador, Guyana, Paraguay, Peru, Suriname, Uruguay, Venezuela

10 MNA Middle East and Northern Africa
Algeria, Bahrain, Egypt, Iran, Iraq, Israel, Jordan, Kuwait, Lebanon, Libya, Morocco, Oman, Qatar, Saudi Arabia, Syrian Arab Republic, Tunisia, United Arab Emirates, Yemen Arab Republic

11 NIS Newly Independent States
Armenia, Azerbaijan, Belarus, Estonia, Georgia, Kazakhstan, Kyrgyz Republic, Latvia, Lithuania, Moldova, Russian Federation, Tajikistan, Turkmenistan, Ukraine, Uzbekistan

12 POE Pacific OECD
Australia, Canada, Korea, Mexico, New Zealand

13 ROW Rest of the World
Bangladesh, Bhutan, Maldives, Nepal, Pakistan, Sri Lanka, Afghanistan, Albania, Andorra, Bosnia-Herzegovina, Brunei, Cambodia, Croatia, Cyprus, Fiji, Kiribati, Laos, Liechtenstein, Macedonia [former Yugoslav Republic of], Malta, Monaco, Mongolia, Myanmar, Nauru, North Korea, Papua New Guinea, San Marino, Solomon Islands, Tonga, Turkey, Tuvalu, Vanuatu, Vietnam, Western Samoa, Yugoslavia [Serbia and Montenegro]

14 SSA Sub-Saharan Africa
Angola, Benin, Botswana, Burkina Faso, Burundi, Cameroon, Cape Verde, Central African Republic, Chad, Comoros, Congo, Côte d'Ivoire, Djibouti, Equatorial Guinea, Eritrea, Ethiopia, Gabon, Gambia, Ghana, Guinea, Guinea-Bissau, Kenya, Lesotho, Liberia, Madagascar, Malawi, Mali, Mauritania, Mauritius, Mozambique, Namibia, Niger, Nigeria, Rwanda, Sao Tome & Principe, Senegal, Seychelles Islands, Sierra Leone, Somalia, South Africa, Sudan, Swaziland, Tanzania, Togo, Uganda, Zaïre, Zambia, Zimbabwe

15 USA United States of America

GDP growth rate
Average annual growth in per cent; based on 1992 PPPs

	1996-2000		2001-2010		2011-2020		1995-2020	
	HG	LG	HG	LG	HG	LG	HG	LG
ASE	7.7	6.1	7.0	4.8	6.4	4.2	6.9	4.8
BRA	5.4	3.8	6.1	3.0	5.1	2.8	5.6	3.1
CHN	9.3	7.9	8.2	5.3	7.2	4.8	8.0	5.6
ECE	5.5	2.0	5.5	3.8	4.0	2.7	4.9	3.0
EUR	2.4	2.4	2.7	2.0	2.1	1.3	2.4	1.8
IDN	7.5	5.9	7.0	4.1	6.7	4.0	7.0	4.4
IND	6.5	4.4	7.2	4.3	6.6	4.2	6.8	4.3
JPN	3.3	3.3	2.9	2.0	2.3	1.2	2.7	1.9
LAT	4.3	3.0	5.9	3.2	5.1	3.1	5.3	3.1
MNA	5.0	2.1	7.1	2.2	6.9	2.2	6.6	2.2
NIS	3.5	1.1	6.0	4.2	6.9	4.0	5.8	3.5
POE	4.3	4.3	4.7	4.0	4.3	3.4	4.5	3.8
ROW	6.5	5.0	6.6	4.3	6.5	4.0	6.5	4.3
SSA	4.6	2.8	5.0	2.8	5.8	2.6	5.2	2.7
USA	2.2	2.2	2.7	2.1	2.6	1.5	2.6	1.9
Total	4.3	3.5	5.0	3.1	4.9	2.8	4.8	3.1
OECD	2.7	2.7	3.0	2.3	2.7	1.6	2.8	2.1
Non-OECD	6.5	4.7	6.9	4.1	6.5	3.9	6.7	4.2
Big Five	7.2	5.4	7.3	4.5	6.7	4.3	7.1	4.6
Other NMEs	5.9	4.0	6.5	3.7	6.2	3.5	6.3	3.7

Source: OECD Estimates.

Population growth rate
Average annual growth in per cent

	1996-2000	2001-2010	2011-2020	1995-2020
ASE	1.54	1.29	0.95	1.20
BRA	1.25	1.15	0.95	1.09
CHN	0.90	0.67	0.60	0.69
ECE	−0.12	−0.08	−0.11	−0.10
EUR	0.21	0.02	−0.09	0.02
IDN	1.49	1.20	0.98	1.17
IND	1.62	1.36	0.99	1.26
JPN	0.22	0.05	−0.26	−0.04
LAT	1.73	1.53	1.27	1.47
MNA	2.40	2.28	1.85	2.13
NIS	0.01	0.07	0.05	0.05
POE	1.27	1.05	0.82	1.00
ROW	2.09	1.80	1.49	1.74
SSA	2.79	2.68	2.45	2.61
USA	0.79	0.74	0.76	0.75
Total	1.38	1.24	1.08	1.21
OECD	0.58	0.44	0.34	0.43
Non-OECD	1.54	1.39	1.21	1.35
Big Five	1.11	0.92	0.74	0.89
Other NMEs	2.16	2.01	1.76	1.94

Source: Population Projections, United Nations, 1996.

CHAPTER 3.   RESPONDING TO POLICY CHALLENGES

The discussion in the preceding chapters lends emphasis to the role of international policy reform in determining the likelihood of alternative growth scenarios. Better domestic policy and a more conducive international environment would enable countries to achieve faster sustainable rates of growth than would otherwise be possible, thus permitting higher standards of living, with a better managed environment as an integral component. Progress on domestic reforms in a number of areas is crucial to reaping fully the benefits of globalisation. Failure to make such progress could threaten a country's integration into the global economy. In the future, large parts of domestic reform agendas of OECD and non-OECD countries will increasingly be pursued in global and regional settings. This chapter examines certain major domestic policy challenges facing OECD and non-OECD countries in coming decades as well as the policy challenges related to the successful integration of the poorest countries in the global economy and to a better management of global resources.

Strengthening competition as a means to stimulate economic growth without weakening shared bonds and attachments of society and community (the solidarity), constitutes a major challenge for OECD governments. Introducing competition to formerly sheltered activities – notably through deregulation of product and services markets, privatisation, anti-monopoly laws and changes in policies and regulations that govern labour and financial markets – is not welcomed by those whose acquired rights are thus modified or eroded, be they individuals, groups of workers or businesses. Solidarity may express itself as a generalised sympathy and support for the threatened interests. Sufficiently widespread, resistance to change can be quite destructive of economic reforms. Experience also shows, however, that understanding and acceptance of the necessity of competition can be created and that determined governments can muster support to push forward with the tough reforms that may be necessary – reduced trade barriers, regulatory reform and privatisation, new labour laws and the like. In many OECD countries, there is a growing constituency for introducing competition to formerly sheltered activities. These topics are taken up in the first section.

The combination of sound macroeconomic, trade and foreign exchange rate policies allied to supportive public investment and encouragement of the private sector has worked well not only in OECD countries but in a growing number of non-OECD countries, led by the dynamic economies of East and Southeast Asia. After a decade of efforts to achieve macroeconomic stability and set up the basic institutional framework for an open market economy, many non-OECD countries now present conditions that are sufficiently similar to those found in dynamic Asia to experience a fast and sustained economic growth. For this to happen, remaining domestic policy challenges such as deepening of market-friendly and pro-innovation policies, achieving further progress with educational attainment, and improving the provision of infrastructure will have to be adequately taken up by non-member governments. The hope is that the rising tide of fast growth in the non-OECD economies will lift enough boats to be the basis for a sustained consensus about policies. Development, however, imposes many cultural and societal strains and there remain considerable risks of marginalisation both of some of the poor groups within society (for example, those living in regions that are by-passed by development) and of whole countries, the latter unable by their own efforts to adjust policies sufficiently far or fast enough to support rapid growth. The policy challenges facing non-OECD countries, notably the poorest, and the evolving role of development co-operation in this context are discussed in the second section.

In recent years, there has been a revival of interest in the question of global resource constraints motivated in large degree by the rapid economic growth of populous countries. In Chapter 2, it was shown that with continued strong agricultural productivity growth the world should be able to produce enough food to feed the population projected for 2020. Most food needs of large economies would continue to be met from domestic production; and increasing imports, notably by China and certain OECD regions, are not expected to cause significant strains on world food markets. It was also shown that energy supplies would likely be adequate to fuel rapid economic growth over the next 25 years without drastic increases in fossil fuel prices. Dependency on Middle East oil suppliers would, however, increase significantly as other low-cost reserves are depleted. Added to this is a dependency of some OECD countries on gas imports from a few countries. The policy challenges related to meeting the fast increasing food needs of developing economies and concerns over future energy security are addressed in the third section.

Environmental pressures also threaten progress, especially over the next quarter-century when many large low income countries will be intensifying their industrial development and making much heavier use of fossil fuels and other polluting inputs. This could more than double global carbon dioxide emissions as well as contributing to regional and local pollution. Pressures on certain renewable resource stocks may also further intensify. If policies can be put in place to deal more effectively with environmental problems, prospects in the longer term are promising. By the second quarter of the century many of these economies will already be shifting towards a less polluting services-intensive economic structure, and the technologies in use will become more and more environment friendly. Moreover, changes in demographic trends and population structure will become more pronounced, and – perhaps most important of all – the great mass of the citizenry, already by 2020 being made considerably better off through economic progress, will be demanding their governments to give environmental measures a higher priority. Many tough issues remain to be tackled, however, and governments will need to find better ways to cope with environmental stresses, global as well as local. The environmental challenges facing Member and non-OECD countries, both separately and in common, are reviewed in the last section, which also discusses the need and scope for closer consultation and international co-operation in this area.

3.1. Policy Challenges in OECD Member Countries

Over the past decade and a half, a progressive shift has occurred in the thrust of economic policies in virtually all OECD countries away from short-term demand management towards medium-term objectives, in particular, establishing the necessary conditions for sustainable non-inflationary growth in productivity and employment. It has become increasingly clear that key macroeconomic problems, notably high unemployment and slow growth, are largely of a structural nature. Despite some progress and limited success in some countries, the policy responses to these macro-structural challenges have to date been insufficient. While price stability has been largely achieved, fiscal positions are now generally worse than in the late 1970s and unemployment remains high. Structural reforms have been significant in the financial sector and international trade, but have lagged in other areas, notably labour and product markets. In part, uneven progress reflects uncertainties about the net benefits and concern about transition costs. Such factors have contributed to political resistance to reform.

OECD countries face a demanding structural reform agenda in coming years, including product market deregulation, social security issues, labour market flexibility, and policies to cope with population ageing. At the same time, efforts by governments to achieve fiscal consolidation will both influence and be influenced by progress in these other areas. For example, lower unemployment would ease fiscal burdens, but additional resources may need to be directed into education and training programmes. Governments in both Europe and North America have indicated a commitment to fiscal consolidation. Those European governments seeking to be in the first EMU wave are aiming to reduce deficits as a share of GDP to 3 per cent by 1998, while the United States aims for budget balance by 2002. Furthermore, governments will need to develop new policies to cope with global environment challenges.

Enhancing competition and innovation through regulatory reform

Many OECD governments have come to recognise the need to reform regulations introduced in another era but rendered obsolete by technological change or seen to stifle competition. By streamlining regulations, de-restricting entry into sectors once reserved as "natural monopolies" and privatising state-owned enterprises, governments can help domestic industry become more cost-efficient and innovative. As noted in Chapter 1, the opening of OECD economies to international trade and investment has exerted a powerful influence on the competitive performance of domestic industries, particularly where domestic producers have historically enjoyed a local monopoly. The greater exposure of domestic producers to competition, through a combination of regulatory and trade reforms, can also serve to strengthen their competitive position in the fast-growing non-member country markets.

Recent OECD work suggests that regulatory reform in a number of key economic sectors could yield significant productivity gains. More heavily regulated countries can expect to see one-time increases in real GDP levels on the order of 3 to 6 per cent after ambitious reform programmes. Countries well-advanced on the path of regulatory reform have already reaped some of those benefits and so stand to gain less from further reform.

Australia assesses its gains from regulatory reform to be around 5.5 per cent of GDP. The European Single Market increased EU income by an estimated 1.5 per cent from 1987 to 1993; and the Commission projects even greater future gains. Japan estimates that reducing pricing and productivity gaps with the United States, primarily through regulatory reform, should increase GDP by several percentage points.

A flow of cost-reducing and productivity-enhancing innovations as well as new product developments are crucial for sustained economic growth. The more effective OECD is as innovator, the better will be the terms on which goods and services from the rest of the world can be obtained. Largely as a result of past responses to competitive pressures, OECD countries are entering a new global age with significant advantages in terms of large stocks of skilled labour and capital (including infrastructure) and well-developed technology and know-how. Also, multinational firms headquartered in OECD countries are responsible for a large share of foreign direct investment and of world trade.

The challenge will be to maintain OECD competitiveness in the face of new pressures both from the rapid changes in technology in prospect and new, stronger competitors, many of whom will be seeking to move upmarket in terms of the technology embodied in their products and services. While most new technology is and will continue to be generated in the OECD area in the coming years, the advantage is short-lived when knowledge is diffused rapidly – and this is increasingly the case as non-OECD countries create more and more receptive conditions to attract global business and upgrade the skills of their own workers.

The further development of innovative capabilities of OECD countries requires a multi-faceted approach from governments. There is a need to sustain the science base, as a source of advanced knowledge on which innovation draws. In a number of OECD countries, R&D expenditures have declined as a share of GDP and in absolute terms in recent years, as a result of the economic slowdown. With economic growth spreading again throughout the OECD area, there are better prospects regarding the private sector's efforts, but government support of R&D risks suffering from continued budget restraints which are being experienced in Member countries. This may have a negative effect on the vitality of basic research which is mostly undertaken in academic institutions, and needs to be supported as a "collective good". Interfaces with industry can be improved by means of various measures such as co-operative R&D centres and well-designed incentives boosting industrial R&D. A better orientation of public and university research to make it more receptive to, and dependent on, industrial demands and funding would also help.

There is also a need in a number of OECD countries, to create a climate that is more conducive to entrepreneurship, by improving access to venture capital, facilitating the mobility of people, and developing a more risk taking culture. While actions concerning the basic education of people, their value systems and the modalities of reward and promotion are important for changing attitudes in the long term, significant results can be obtained in the short term by removing all forms of bureaucratic obstacles and seeking to reverse anti-competitive behaviour.

Pressures to reform social policy

Judged by common social indicators, OECD Member countries can look back to a very impressive post-World War II record in all main areas of social policy: health, education and housing standards have risen substantially; social protection and income support has become much more "generous" and the work-leisure balance has improved rather dramatically for most people. Despite major economic restructuring, employment and family income have grown, if not always as smoothly and to the extent desired. In the face of rigid labour market behaviour and changing labour supply and demand conditions – on the supply side the coincidence of the advent of the post-war baby boom generation on the labour market and strongly rising female participation rates, and on the demand side the impact of restrictive policies to combat inflationary pressure and to restore sound fiscal balance – unemployment has grown to uncomfortably high levels in many countries, but social programmes have served to ease many of the resulting financial problems.

Yet, discussions of social policy are generally not marked by a sense of complacency. There is a widespread feeling that existing arrangements, at existing levels of funding, cannot – or should not – be continued. Pressures for change arise in several contexts: public finance, the capacity to handle new problems and a looming threat to living standards of parts of the population.

Fiscal pressures: social programmes are inevitably affected as governments strive to reduce deficits and debts. Figure 3.1 shows the large proportion of GDP that is devoted to public social spending, although with seemingly large variations across OECD Member countries. Despite recent cut-backs in many social programmes, total social costs are rising and are expected to continue to rise in coming years – dramatically in some cases – as a result of the effects of population ageing on the cost of pensions and health care. The result will be even less capacity for spending in other high priority areas,

◆ Figure 3.1. **Public sector social outlays in relation to GDP, 1993**

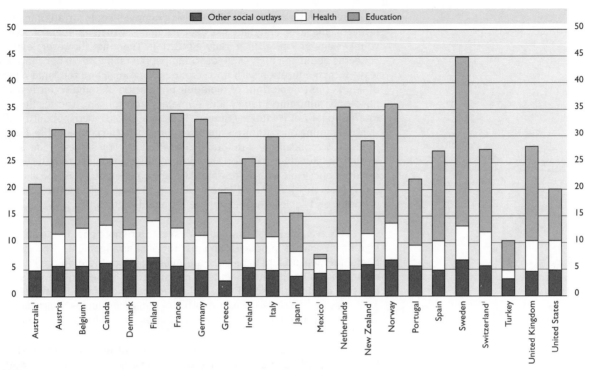

| | Other social outlays | Health | Education |

1. 1992
Note: The differences among countries are reduced when allowance is made for factors such as taxation of benefits, mandatory requirements for employers to provide benefits, or tax subsidies for private provision. If private spending on health is included, the differences among countries are considerably narrowed again.
Source: OECD Social and Education Expenditures Data Bases.

such as problems associated with poor children, and other social areas that are not currently funded.

In principle, it should be possible to re-allocate spending from less useful social programmes to more effective ones. However, this has not proved easy within existing structures. For example, there have been real advances in health care, but the relationship between health care spending and health outcomes is not always empirically well established. Indeed, in most social areas, effectiveness is simply not measured in any systematic fashion. Little is known about the effects of interventions in the medical, educational, training or labour market fields when these are taken in different combinations or sequences.

In short, in the absence of reform, existing arrangements, which tend to rely on high levels of public spending, are unlikely to meet future social needs. Indeed, the main public finance debate is about the extent to which the added age-related costs can, or should, continue to be financed from the public purse.

Pressures to overcome rigidities in work, learning and leisure: while the parallel growth in leisure, employment and educational attainment may be seen as a typical and welcome feature of "affluent societies", there have been rigidities in the allocation of life time spent or devoted to these three areas that are not easy to deal with under existing arrangements. Reform would be needed quite independent of public finance pressures.

Leisure has increased in total, dramatically so in the case of retirement. However, work and leisure have not been allocated in a flexible way, with especially worrisome rigidities in the work-to-retirement transition. As will be discussed below, the result is a serious threat to future living standards.

Skills and learning provide another example. People are attaining higher levels of education and there has been a large growth in numbers of people in younger age groups with tertiary education. There are, however, legitimate concerns about the high share of young people (some 15-20 per cent) which leave formal education with no useful qualifications, and the large numbers of adults (up to one third of the adult population of some countries) which have only minimum literacy and numeracy according to the results of the International Adult Literacy Survey. There are also concerns about rigidities in how learning opportunities are distributed over the course of life. Learning tends to be concentrated in formal education at early stages of life, and not enough at later stages. Lifelong learning for all is needed so that the economy can draw on people with up-to-date skills and competencies. This would enable individuals at all skill and income levels to play a productive role in the economy and society throughout their longer lifetimes.

However, lifelong learning for all seems a remote goal in the absence of significant change in policies and institutional arrangements. The most fundamental measures to achieve it are missing. Also, there are no consistent means of comparing the benefits that result from higher skill levels with the costs of acquiring those skills in various formal and informal settings. In the absence of such information, "investing in human resources" must remain an abstract objective rather than a practical strategy for allocating resources.

Similarly, employment has grown in recent decades – in most cases keeping up with, and even surpassing, the growth in the size of the working-age population. However, jobs have been re-allocated in ways that were not anticipated when the welfare state was first put in place after World War II. Employment has increased dramatically among women. This has been a major factor in maintaining family incomes. However, it also has resulted in adjustment problems in the provision of child care and early childhood development, and highlighted problems about social arrangements for single parents. At the same time, there has been a reallocation of employment away from young people and older workers in most countries. There is a growing gap between those who are well placed to profit from the new career opportunities created by globalisation and those who are not. Joblessness and low wages can re-inforce a complex of social problems, including, for example, those associated with crime, inner city decay and family instability. There are fears of growing polarisation and a threat to social cohesion.

These examples illustrate the importance of overcoming rigidities in the allocation of life time spent in work, learning, care-giving and leisure (policy responses are known as active ageing policies), and of effective investments in human resources. Although there are many exceptions, traditional policies and institutions are too fragmented – and not sufficiently based on evidence of what works – to address these issues adequately. Indeed, often they create unintended barriers and contribute to rigidity.

Pressures of ageing population on future living standards: the effects of population ageing, compounded by the ageing of the baby boom generation, are large, well known and tend to dominate the public debate. Figure 3.2 compares the ratio of older people to the working-age population in 1990 with projections for 2020. These ratios are already large and will grow dramatically, especially in countries such as Japan. Less well understood are the changes that are taking place through a combination of increased longevity and changing life-course patterns. The extent of these changes is evident by simply converting familiar labour force survey data to a life basis. Figure 3.3 shows, for example,

◆ Figure 3.2. **Elderly dependency ratios (65+/active pop.): 1990 and 2020, OECD countries**
(percentage)

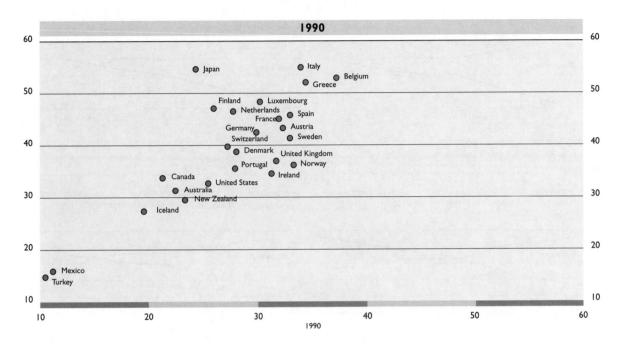

Note: 2020 active population is estimated from 2020 population of working age multiplied by 2010 participation rate.
Source: Based on ILO database.

that a boy born in Australia in 1975 would expect to live, on average, to age 70. Given a continuation of the labour market situation prevalent then, 44 of those 70 years would be expected to be spent in paid employment. The remaining 26 years would be spent in other ways-in school, retirement, unemployment, etc. An Australian boy born in 1995 could expect to live to age 75, a large increase in life expectancy. Of those 75 years, there will be an almost even split between the amount of life spent in employment and the amount spent outside of employment, mainly in school and retirement. The extent of the shift varies from country to country and is, of course, influenced by current labour market conditions. However, in all cases, there is a rapid, fundamental shift in the structure of society.

In short, there will be comparatively fewer people working to pay for the pension and health costs of a much greater number of retirees. Unless there are additional imports, financed by retirees' or pension funds' foreign assets (see Sections 1.3 and 2.5), the amount of goods and services that will be available to be purchased by the population will have to be produced by a relatively smaller group of workers. This implies that either real disposable income of workers will have to be lower than in case of former lifetime patterns or retirees would receive less. Most likely both would occur. There is no escape from this simple arithmetic. Some people, especially those with higher incomes and savings, may be quite pleased to trade-off increased leisure in retirement for a reduction in consumption. However, the main result is likely to be hardship for many. More productivity in work, reduced unemployment, greater participation by women or more migration will certainly help easing the transfer burden. However, the fundamental solution must involve a reversal of trends in lifetime spending patterns and lifetime work-leisure distribution.

◆ Figure 3.3. **Expected years in employment and not in employment for men in selected OECD countries**
(expected years)

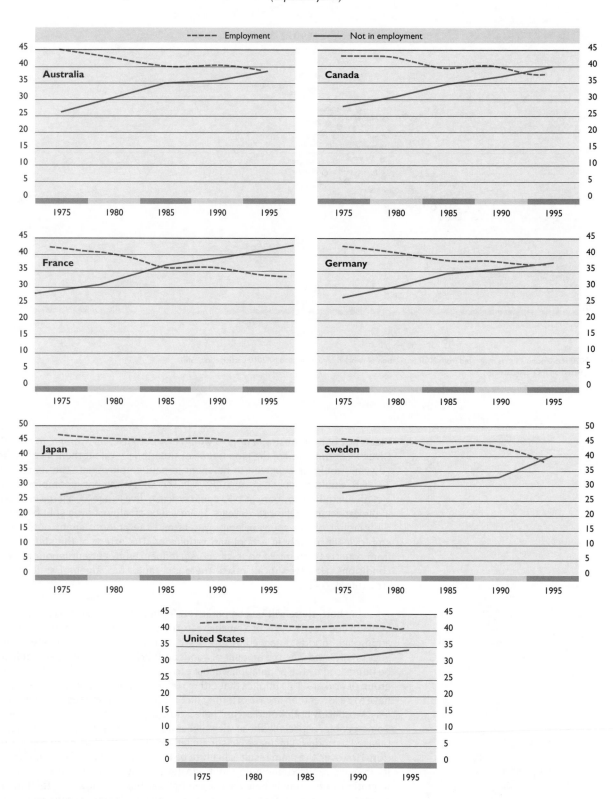

Source: OECD Labour Force Statistic, Part III.
          United Nations "World Population Prospects 1950-2050 (The 1996 revision)".

Increased life expectancy under better health conditions therefore calls for people to be prepared to work longer and remain productive, to save more during working life, and to cover more of their expenditure on health and care. A complex reform agenda will be needed to support these changes, an agenda that will eventually transform social policy. Action is required on pensions, health and care, and education and training to support skills and productivity as people age. Moreover, incentives that encourage early retirement must be removed, and financial market regulation reformed to encourage more productive savings.

Social programmes reflect a particular balance of individual and collective responsibilities. This is a balance of costs, benefits and risks among individuals, families, generations, service providers, governments and other organisations. Taken as a whole, social programmes and institutions have not kept pace with the rapid change that is taking place in this balance. A catch-up is needed and that will not be simple.

The model of society underlying most social programming no longer applies today. For example, most public policies in OECD countries still assume that people pass through three quite separate stages of life. Education is almost exclusively for the young. Pensions provide a separate secure stream of income security for older people and old age is often associated with growing infirmity. In the middle years, there are stable jobs and families, typically with one earner in a family. Social protection programmes provide income for the exceptional times when this stability is missing. Financing of these programmes assumes that full-time, steady jobs are the norm. The real world never did fully conform to these simple assumptions. However, they were sufficiently valid to provide the basis for government programming that worked fairly well in most Member countries through the 1950s, 1960s and into the 1970s.

Today, however, societies in most OECD counties have moved a long distance towards a different model. The age-structure in many countries is beginning to resemble a cylinder more than a pyramid. There are more parents and grandparents to support fewer numbers of children. There are growing numbers of retired people in their 60s and 70s who share many of the same health and social characteristics as adults in middle age and below. Even greater growth is projected in the number of the very old who do experience frailty.

As noted, there have been major shifts in time spent in work, learning and leisure. Changing employment structures have meant that many more people than originally envisaged have come to rely on government income support. Further, income support, alone, is not the answer in helping people find new jobs.

Social programmes are still mainly based on the old set of assumptions. As a result they may inadvertently send wrong signals. Some programmes, for example, may create disincentives to work or may undervalue the role of families and community. The growth in two-earner families makes a big difference in the nature of the social contract. For example, both gainfully employed family members may be required to make contributions to programmes which provide benefits that neither really needs. Traditional social insurance arrangements, which assume that each generation makes its way into working-life, do not cover the risk that children may not be able to establish themselves in their careers. Some programmes have become so complex that their effects are often not transparent. Inter-generational effects are rarely taken into account and reforms designed to reduce beneficiaries of one programme may simply result in shifting people to other programmes. This has been the experience with invalidity benefits in many countries.

A growing misalignment between social programmes and emerging social realities may result in a loss of faith in the viability of the social contract. Many young people, for example, do not believe that adequate public pensions will be paid to them when they retire. An increasing number of families may feel they will get less out of the State than they contribute to finance social programmes, with a resulting resistance to tax increases and growing distrust in government. In an environment of increasing income inequality, polarisation will grow further.

There is also a widespread tendency for governments to rely on costly remedial programmes rather than preventive measures where more responsibility is on the individual and family. Individuals may be treated in a fragmented way – as holders of entitlements to specific benefits or as clients of specific services. The providers of services are fragmented across disciplines, and policy-making is fragmented across government departments. Taken as a whole, existing programming does not recognise the commonality among the determinants of health, learning capability, individual productivity, income, crime, and general well-being. Policies rarely take account of the well-documented fact that what happens to people at one stage of life can make a big difference at later stages.

The long-run effects of desirable reform would be large. As the reform process itself can, for the most part, be based on incremental change, reform would seem quite manageable if sensible action is taken early. The underlying trends are favourable: people are living longer and healthier lives, and are becoming more skilled. The potential therefore exists for people to make greater contributions to the society and the economy at large. There could be greater returns on investments in human resource development, as people can apply their skills over a longer time period. Population ageing is also decreasing the relative size of the working-age population which, along with economic recovery, should reduce unemployment and make it easier for people to work longer.

Much of the required change will take place almost automatically as individuals and organisations adjust their spending patterns to new situations. Popuageing has been taking place for some time and changes of behaviour are evolving in response. For example, people are saving more for retirement, as reflected in more rapid growth of pension fund assets. Policies are also evolving: the growth of health care costs has been curtailed; pension reforms have been introduced; and work disincentives embodied in many social programmes have been removed or reduced. Many programmes that directly encouraged early retirement have been dropped. While the effects of some of these reforms will be minor in light of the magnitude of the challenge, they are nevertheless steps in the right direction.

The basic timetable for action by governments is driven by the ageing of the baby-boom generation as it moves towards retirement. This gives a window of opportunity for further reform. In most countries, the largest effects of population ageing will not be felt for well over a decade. In order to prepare for the future, it is important, however, to accelerate the pace of reform and to build consensus around a reform strategy. Areas where adjustment may occur without major government action, or where reform is likely to have the highest pay-off, must be identified as well as areas for early action. The latter are likely to include the following:

– ensuring the sustainability of pension promises while keeping budgetary costs manageable in light of fiscal pressures;

– acting now so that ages of entitlement to retirement benefits would rise on a gradual basis with ample advance notice, thereby easing the transition period to a longer working life;

– beginning to collect the data needed to ensure the effectiveness of reforms.

There is no single reform strategy that would be suitable for all economies and situations alike. Action depends on the social and economic situation of each country, its values and institutions, and its present programming mix. However, since the underlying pressures for change are similar across countries, there will be many common elements in reforms.

Retirement: Although the reform process is well launched, the key challenge in many countries will be to continue efforts to put the financing of retirement income, health and chronic care on a sustainable basis in light of the pressures that population ageing will pose. The longer reform is delayed, the more painful solutions will become. Reform is not only a fiscal matter. As noted in a recent OECD study on ageing (see Annex: "Notes on the sources"), "it is also about the extent to which, in an uncertain world, the spending choices of coming generations will be pre-empted. Inaction on pension reform locks away an increasing share of GDP for decades to come. Coming generations may have more important priorities than allocating ever-increasing shares of national income to support ever-increasing amounts of leisure at the end of life."

Figure 3.4 illustrates the potential scope of possible reforms to public pensions. For the year 2020, it compares a baseline (which assumes no pensions changes except those already announced) with a scenario where the average

◆　Figure 3.4.　**Pension expenditures in 1995 and 2020 (various scenarios)**
(percentage of GDP in 1994 prices)

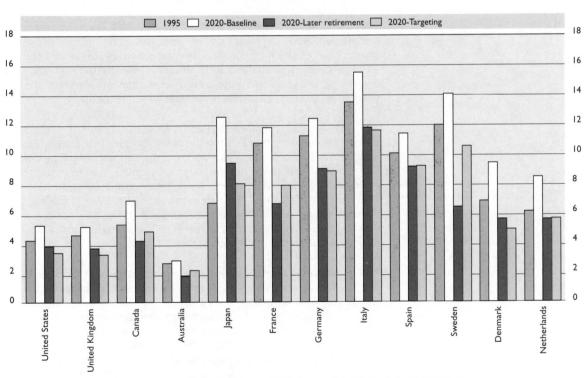

Source: Based on scenario estimates developed in OECD (1996), "Ageing in OECD Countries", *Social Policy Studies No. 20,* Table 2.3.

effective age of retirement is gradually increased to age 70 and another "targeting" scenario where public pensions are gradually reduced to a point where they eventually cover only 30 per cent of the population. The results of these computations must be treated carefully. In reality, countries do change pension arrangements periodically and the "baseline" is therefore only a hypothetical (and unlikely) case. As well, reforms typically take place on a variety of fronts, and should take account of other elements of the retirement income system as well as public pensions. Nevertheless, the chart gives a rough indication of the scale of the challenge and the wide variety of situations in different countries.

As noted earlier, the fundamental direction for reform must be increased flexibility in the work-retirement transition and a reversal in trends of spending increasing periods of life in retirement. Success here will also have positive repercussions on a range of other social and economic areas. Overall success depends on reducing work disincentives in the whole tax-transfer system, on the health and skills of people to work productively throughout their prolonged working life, and the opportunities to acquire the necessary skills. It also implies that there are appropriate pay practices that do not artificially increase the costs of retaining older workers, and that labour market flexibility encompasses suitable hours and working-life arrangements as well as wages.

Public debate on pensions too often presents issues as an either/or choice between different types of arrangements. This can be unhelpful if it takes attention away from the central long-term issue: slowing or reversing trends towards more time spent in retirement. Moreover, it may put an artificial cast on the practical process of reform, where consensus is usually easier to find by making modifications to existing arrangements. An important element of practical reform strategies is finding the right balance among the various elements of the retirement income system. Resources available on retirement typically include various types of funded and pay-as-you-go pensions, private savings, assets such as housing, and income from informal employment. From the perspective of risk diversification, a larger number of sources of retirement income makes sense. Each of the elements has strengths and weakness and the correct balance will depend on the current situation in a country. That situation will evolve over the years and there is much to recommend a system where small changes to a variety of pillars is the best way of responding.

In most OECD countries, the trend towards placing greater weight on funded elements is likely to continue. There has been rapid growth in pension fund assets and these are expected to grow even more dramatically in coming decades. In most countries, there are likely to be consequential changes in the regulatory environment for financial markets. Though not social policies, such reforms are important for strengthening the financial basis of retirement income systems. There could be large global consequences if reforms encourage mutually-advantageous investments of OECD pension fund assets in the non-OECD world, raising overall rates of return (see Section 2.5).

Human resource development will be another central theme in reform-development of cost-effective, accessible ways of acquiring and maintaining relevant skills over the course of life for people of all skill levels. Again, there are wide social and economic implications. On the economic side, human resource development is key to strategies for improving productivity, competitiveness in the global economy and job growth. On the social side, it is central to dealing with the problem of joblessness and poverty. Low incomes are often a reflection of low skill levels.

Reform priorities often include improved access to early childhood education and revitalising schools. They include better linkages between work and learning and creating incentives to invest more in lifelong learning. A central challenge will be to find ways to measure and recognise skills acquired outside formal education and training institutions. Another will be to find ways of ensuring that people with low skills and income get greater opportunities to invest in skills and take advantage of them.

Valuing care-giving, learning as well as paid work. Too often social and economic policies look at the world in terms of a simple trade-off between having, or not having, paid work. Ways and means need to be found to measure and value contributions made in other domains of life: voluntary activities, care of children and the frail elderly in the family, and learning in its many facets and dimensions. These domains are important in their own right–especially so since paid work is occupying a relatively smaller part of life. They have also important implications for economic and social policies.

Cost effectiveness. Effort can be advanced in making social programmes more cost-effective before the baby-boom generation retires. This will be particularly important in managing health and chronic care costs. The past record of success in measuring cost-effectiveness has not been high. However, new information technology, which is only now becoming available, will eventually help in planning and delivering services based on information about their likely subsequent outcomes. For example, it may become possible to categorise some types of social spending as investments, with spending levels determined on the basis of expected future returns. Medical research, active labour market programming and some health interventions would fit in this category. Other programming – examples include many health interventions, chronic care or support for active living by older people – provides services that have value in their own right. Better information about which of these work best will help determine candidates for additional public or private spending, and will help in deciding which should be dropped. Better data on results would also lead to greater sharing of information, in and among OECD and non-OECD countries, on lessons to be learned and best practices. Such information could also help re-invigorate institutional reforms (such as incorporation of market incentives or various service quality initiatives), by allowing a more objective assessment of their success. While it is difficult to predict the timing and ultimate success of such a shift towards cost-effectiveness, potential gains are large.

Preventive/remedial balance. Another direction of reform is likely to be more preventive programming, reducing the need for subsequent remedial interventions. An emphasis on prevention means greater focus on interventions at earlier stages of life, and more problematic cases, such as income support for low-income families with young children. More attention will have to be devoted to interventions at transition points in life – neo-natal, school-work, work-retirement, or the onset of frailty. More attention given to public information will allow existing services to be better used. Examples are the electronic labour exchange or routine provision of public information about best approaches to training, nutrition or retirement savings.

Remedial programming will, of course, always remain an important part of social policy. There will always be a minority of people who face barriers to an independent life in the market, in families and communities as a result of sickness, low skills, physical or mental disabilities, or lack of family support. In a re-balanced social contract, remedial programming will be designed to support those who need help most, without creating a general culture of dependency. Reforms in this direction should make interventions less fragmented and more centred on the needs of specific individuals. They will recognise that vulnerability at an earlier stage of life, unless timely addressed, risks leading to subsequent and generally more complex problems. More attention must be paid to early identification of problems, the use of case-management techniques in helping people find solutions and, as noted above, the use of statistical information to determine the characteristics – and sequence – of interventions that are likely to work best.

Individual and collective responsibilities. A shift towards more preventive programming represents a re-balancing of the social contract by encouraging and inducing individuals and families to make their own decisions, thereby reducing the need for collective, remedial interventions. Other elements in the rebalancing of individual and collective responsibilities will include new policy approaches to fairness and risk over the course of life of individual persons. Many pension plans have already been reformed to create a tighter linkage of contributions and benefits. Treating long-term care for frail elderly people as a normal life risk is another example. So are proposals to create larger pools of individual savings – or paid leave entitlements – so that they can be put to a more flexible mix of uses such as care or education leave. Another example is programming that automatically targets benefits to individuals at times of life when they are most needed, while requiring contributions by the individual during periods when income is higher. Refundable income tax credits are one example. Another would involve shifting more of the burden of post-secondary financing to graduates who have benefited from it in terms of a higher earnings stream.

In summary, deep changes can be anticipated in social policy over coming decades as reforms keep up with rapidly changing social realities. The particular nature of the reforms will vary depending on country circumstances, but because similar challenges are being faced, there will be many common themes in these reforms – and much opportunity for sharing of lessons learned among OECD and non-OECD countries.

3.2. Policy Challenges in Non-OECD Countries

An emerging policy consensus

A brief glance at the record of the twenty-five years ending 1995 (see Figure 3.5) shows that only a handful of non-OECD countries have sustained high GDP growth rates – averaging 5 per cent per annum or more throughout this period. The outstanding performers remain the fast-growing countries of East and Southeast Asia, whose success owes much to sound macroeconomic policies (price stability, realistic real exchange and real interest rates, low fiscal deficits), outward orientation, reliance on private sector development, investments in human capital and strong market institutions. Amongst countries that have shown some improvement in their economic performance in the past decade, the most dramatic case is Chile, where competition-enhancing policy reforms have been quite far-reaching; and to a lesser extent India where the recent acceleration of growth can also be largely attributed to a reform push that began in the mid-1980s and has gained momentum since 1991. For most developing countries, there has been little change of economic fortunes over the past quarter century, with growth rates well under 5 per cent. Many have seen little or no improvement in per capita incomes over the period, and, for more than a few, living standards have fallen.

The East Asian experience and a mounting volume of empirical evidence from other countries suggests that linkage-enhancing policies have not only been good for growth, but also for poverty alleviation and social security improvements. In a set of poor countries, mainly in Asia, which over the past three decades oriented their economies towards dynamic participation in world trade, investment and technology flows, a profound transformation of living standards has been achieved. The results are not so surprising since *sustainable* growth requires an intensive use of the factors in relative abundance in the economy in question which, for most poor countries, means low-skilled labour. While a range of very different economies, from Indonesia to Singapore to the Republic of Korea, have made major inroads against poverty, no case is more

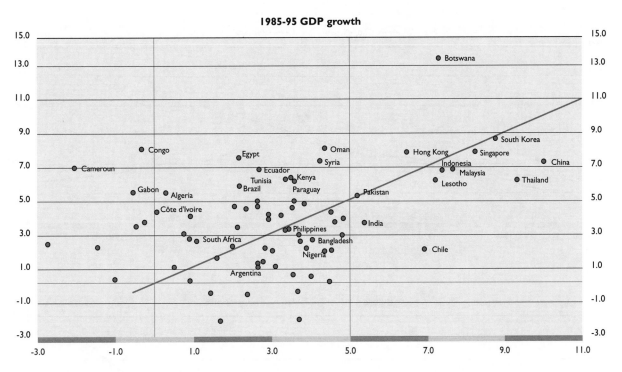

◆ Figure 3.5. **Real GDP growth (per cent per annum)**
(percentage)

1985-95 GDP growth

Source: World Bank, STARS Database.

dramatic than that of China, with its population of nearly 1.2 billion. In 1978, at the onset of its economic reforms, some 60 per cent of its people lived in poverty (defined as per capita daily income, at PPPs, of one US dollar or less). By 1994, just over a fourth remained below the poverty line. In sharp contrast, the poverty reduction record has been disappointing and even negative in those countries, whether relatively advanced or relatively poor, that remained too long with economic policies and structures unfriendly to market forces and international trade and investment. This comparison holds even allowing for the terms of trade and financial shocks that exerted powerful effects on developing economies in the 1970s and 1980s. Countries with similar economic structures and income levels fared very differently in growth, poverty reduction and income distribution according to whether or not their policy orientation was geared to succeeding in international markets and, where appropriate, diversifying away from primary commodities to manufactures (for a comparison of selected African and Asian countries, see Figure 3.6 and Table 3.1).

Despite recent progress with poverty reduction, latest estimates of extreme poverty suggest a world total of some 1.3 billion people, roughly 30 per cent of the world population. India (450 million) and China (350 million) account for over 60% of the total; adding other Big Five countries gives a Big Five total of 900 million. Sub-Saharan Africa is the other major area of poverty, accounting for some 220 million. Faster growth such as that associated with the HG scenario would reduce significantly these distressingly large numbers (for example, assuming an unchanged income distribution, the proportion of those living in absolute poverty would become negligible in China and would fall by three-fourths in India). For the HG scenario to materialise, however, policy challenges facing non-OECD economies need to be adequately addressed by their governments.

◆ Figure 3.6. **Real GDP per capita**
(1987 US$)

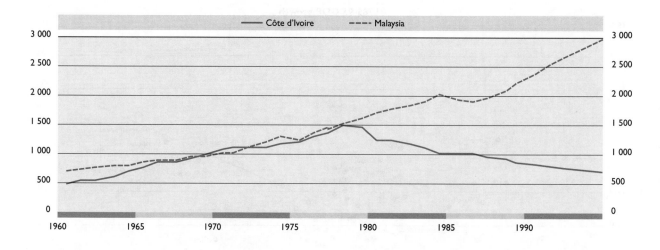

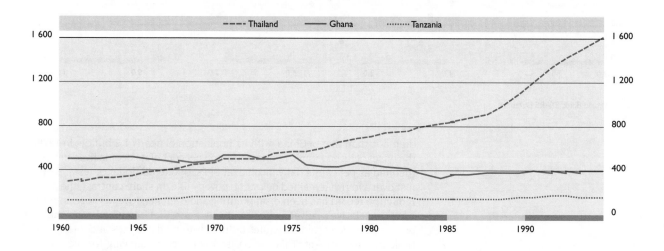

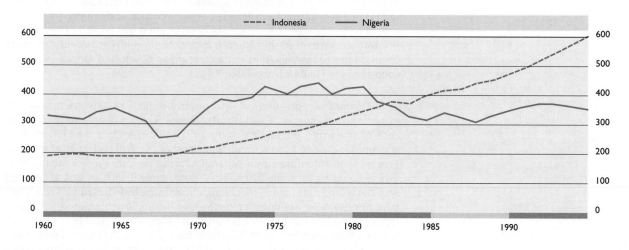

Source: The World Bank, STARS Data Base.

Table 3.1. **Selected economic indicators for seven African and Asian countries**

	Agriculture		Industry		Services	
	1970	1995	1970	1995	1970	1995
Structure of production (%)						
Malaysia	29	13	25	43	46	44
Côte d'Ivoire	40	30	23	20	37	50
Thailand	26	11	25	40	49	49
Tanzania	41	58	17	17	42	24
Ghana	47	46	18	16	35	38
Indonesia	45	17	19	42	36	41
Nigeria	41	28	14	53	45	19

	Fuels, minerals and metals		Other primary commodities		Manufactures	
	1970	1992	1970	1992	1970	1992
Structure of merchandise exports (%)						
Malaysia	30	14	63	21	7	65
Côte d'Ivoire	2	11	92	79	6	10
Thailand	15	2	77	32	8	66
Tanzania	7	4	80	81	13	15
Ghana	13	15	86	84	1	1
Indonesia	44	38	54	15	1	47
Nigeria	62	96	36	3	1	1

Source: STARS Data Base and World Development Report 1994, The World Bank.

Over the past decade, many reforming economies have made great progress in the battle against macroeconomic instability. Trade and investment have been substantially liberalised, though far more so in some countries than in others. Tables 3.2 and 3.3 show for the Big Five economies some indicators of progress with macroeconomic stabilisation and trade opening. In Brazil and Russia, inflation has fallen dramatically from early 1990s levels. While three of the five still have sizeable fiscal deficits, two (India and Russia) have been narrowing the deficit. In the first half of the 1990s, export growth has accelerated in all of the Big Five relative to the 1980s. Brazil and India still have rather low trade-to-GDP ratios, but these could be expected to rise as the effects of recent trade reforms are more widely felt.

Table 3.2. **Macroeconomic indicators for the 1990s**
Per cent

	GDP[a]		Inflation		Current account[c]		Fiscal balance[c]	
	90-95	96-98	90-95	96-98	90-95	96-98	90-95	96-98
Brazil	2.6	3.8	98.6	11.1	−0.5	−3.2	−3.1[b]	−4.3
China	11.8	9.8	9.7	6.6	1.8	−1.4	−2.1	..
India	3.8	5.4	9.8	8.2	−1.3	−1.7	−6.6	−5.9
Indonesia	7.6	7.2	9.0	7.5	−2.8	−1.7	0.4	..
Russia	−9.3	0.9	514.4	17.0	1.9	0.7	-9.5[b]	−4.5

a) Average annual growth rate.
b) 1993-1995.
c) Per cent of GDP.
Source: OECD Economic Outlook.

Table 3.3. **Trade growth and trade/GDP ratios**
Percentage

	Export growth[a]		Trade/GDP ratio	
	1980-90	1990-95	1980	1995
Brazil	6.1	8.2	19.0	14.4
China	11.4	19.1	18.8	42.2
India	6.3	11.2	13.6	17.7
Indonesia	5.3	12.1	41.9	41.2
Russia	..	17.4[b]	..	39.0

a) Annual average growth at current prices and exchange rate.
b) 1992-1995.
Source: Based on *World Development Indicators*, The World Bank.

Future challenges facing non-OECD countries

Non-OECD governments can now focus their attention on the most challenging reform agenda: the completion of domestic deregulation of both product and factor markets, reduction of the state's direct production activities through further privatisation and strengthening of the financial sector. These broad challenges resemble those facing OECD countries, to wit, fostering competition while maintaining social cohesion. In various specifics, however, important differences remain. In some large non-OECD economies, market institutions and the framework of law are of quite recent origin and require further strengthening, and property rights are not deeply entrenched. The educational attainment of the population in most non-OECD countries still lags quite far behind the OECD countries (see Table 3.4) and in some there are still wide gender gaps. Higher investments in education will be necessary over extended periods if the education gap, including the gender gap, is to be narrowed significantly.

Table 3.4. **Educational attainment in selected non-OECD regions and countries[a]**

	Average years of schooling		Growth rate, Years of schooling
	1960	1994	1960-94
China	1.7	5.3	3.5
Indonesia	1.1	5.0	4.5
Other Dynamic Asia	2.7	7.2	3.0
Malaysia	2.3	7.0	3.3
Philippines	3.8	7.4	2.0
Singapore	3.0	6.1	2.1
Thailand	3.5	7.5	2.3
Chinese Taipei	3.2	8.2	2.8
South Asia	1.3	3.4	2.8
Africa	1.6	3.5	2.4
Middle East	1.4	4.9	3.8
Latin America	3.0	5.5	1.8
OECD	**7.3**	**9.8**	**0.9**

a) Computed using the 88 country sample. Regional averages are calculated by weighting each country by its average GDP over 1960-94, as measured in 1985 dollars.
b) Annual percentage rate.
Source: Collins and Bosworth (1996), "Economic Growth in East Asia: Accumulation versus Assimilation", *Brookings Papers on Economic Activity*, 2:135-191.

Moreover, many non-OECD countries have grossly inadequate infrastructure, which severely constrains the growth process, adds significantly to the costs of doing business and discourages both foreign and local investment. Fortunately, new means of mobilising private financing in infrastructure have emerged in recent years, and the timeframe for plugging infrastructure gaps has narrowed drastically (*e.g.*, by contracting independent power providers to build and operate new, scaleable power plants).

Challenges differ depending on region and level of development. For the low-income, populous countries of Asia and Africa, promoting job-creating growth will remain a top priority in the years ahead. Further progress on linkage-oriented reforms and the dismantling of remaining policy biases against agriculture will be necessary. While these should provide a more conducive environment for growth, they will need to be accompanied by major initiatives to extend further the benefits of basic education and literacy, narrowing the rural-urban and male-female education gaps. In the longer run, higher rates of female education will also have an important influence on fertility. Also, greater investment in rural infrastructure is essential to bringing the farmer in closer contact with urban and overseas markets.

In Latin America, securing macroeconomic stability and its benefits remains a high priority, followed by various reforms to introduce greater competition in domestic product markets and flexibility in factor markets. Financial sector reform is high on the agenda in several countries, as is the reform of government finances to reduce government debt levels and provide more room for private investment. One particularly difficult challenge facing Latin America concerns how to deal with the legacy of wide disparities in income and wealth distribution. Recent work suggests several possible links between income distribution and growth. An initially low level of income inequality can foster social cohesion as well as political and macroeconomic stability. Where inequality is high, ensuring social cohesion may require strong redistributive policies, which, depending on the specific measures, can distort economic incentives and retard growth. In East Asia, at least two factors underpinned the relatively flat income distribution at the onset of rapid growth: prior land reform and high levels of investment in universal primary education. In Latin America, the political feasibility of the former is doubtful and, in any case, a very high proportion of the population (including the poor) are city-dwellers. Educational reform to redress the longstanding bias favouring higher education to the neglect of quality at lower levels holds the greatest promise.

Through much of their high-growth catch-up phase, the DAEs have relied heavily on borrowing, imitating and adapting products and processes developed in more advanced countries. To varying degrees, they continue to do this. However, with the narrowing of the technology gap by the more developed among them – they have had to rely more on their own technological resources. Heavy investments over the past couple of decades in higher education have built up a human capital base that should ease the transition. At the same time, industrial enterprises in the DAEs are having to invest larger shares of their profits in research and development (R&D) activities and, in several countries, public R&D investments have also risen steeply to support the process of technology upgrading. The rapid expansion of patent registrations in the United States by Chinese Taipei and the Republic of Korea (see Table 3.5) indicates an acceleration of innovative activity. For large developing economies, productivity catch-up will continue to rely mostly on technological borrowing, from both the DAEs and the OECD countries. As they undertake more of their own R&D investments, the most advanced non-OECD countries will share increasingly the interest of the OECD countries in a well-defined and enforced international system of intellectual property rights to ensure that those investments are adequately rewarded.

Table 3.5.   **Number of patents granted in the United States**

	1980	1989	1995
USA	37 124	50 134	55 588
Japan	7 136	20 177	21 795
Germany	5 802	8 332	6 610
France	2 096	3 139	2 821
Great Britain	2 416	3 103	2 503
NIS	463	161	127
China	1	53	71
Brazil	25	36	63
India	5	15	40
Indonesia	1	5	4
Chinese Taipei	69	594	1 626
Rep. of Korea	10	160	1 166
Hong Kong	28	50	92
Singapore	4	19	53

Source: OECD Data Base.

For many non-OECD economies, a long-term issue of great consequence is the profound changes in society and possibly culture that globalisation and the modernisation of economic structures likely will bring in their wake. One important aspect of such change is the evolving role of women as they achieve higher levels of education and enter the paid labour force. Another is the further shift towards urban settlement patterns and lifestyles (see Box 3.1), though this – like the ongoing demographic transition – has already had a marked impact in most parts of the developing world. Still another is the evolving role of government in societies becoming much more open to information than in the past, with a populace that is better educated and likely both to be more critical and vocal in regard to the performance of public officials and to play a more active role in governance as democratic systems take root in much of the world.

Integrating the poorest into the global economy

The complex domestic foundations of successful integration into the world economy explain why linkage-based development is no easy achievement. Because the challenges and opportunities are always country specific, each nation has to find its own way. This invariably involves a major effort of political leadership to overcome social obstacles and rigidities, and to reform areas of major economic dysfunction. New "success stories" are emerging on all continents as progress is made with the basic policy challenges, and the dynamic gains from international trade, investment and technology begin to boost economic performance. Concerns have been raised, however, about the marginalisation of poor countries and poor people, particularly in backward regions of large countries, that is occuring as a consequence of globalisation.

While outward-oriented policies like trade and investment liberalisation are essential to integration with the world economy, avoiding marginalisation requires broader progress with the fundamentals of development. Particular attention must be paid to:

– the development of an effective governance system under the rule of law, an active civil society, and a capacity to manage internal conflicts;

Box 3.1. Urbanisation in Non-OECD Economies

To an increasing extent, the population of the non-OECD world is urban. In 1990, UN estimates indicate that some 34 per cent of the population of less developed countries was urban while projections suggest that the 50 per cent threshold would be crossed a little before 2020. Latin America has long been the most heavily urbanised region outside the OECD and there the urban population share is already about 75 per cent. For the future, urban growth is expected to be particularly rapid in Asia though the urban areas of Africa may also grow quickly. Accompanying the growth of the urban population is an increase in the size and number of so-called megacities (cities with a population of 10 million or more inhabitants); as of the mid-1990s, there were 12 such megacities, including 6 located outside the OECD. Over the next twenty years there may be as many as 28 megacities, most located in Asia.

Changing patterns of occupation that mirror the changes in output structure in favour of industry and services account for part of the move to cities and towns. Even in predominantly rural areas, the increase in marketed agricultural produce, the growth of industries based on processing of agricultural materials, and the growing needs for agricultural services, machinery and repair facilities can lead to burgeoning growth of rural towns and market centres. In locations particularly favoured as global centres – often port cities or those otherwise having very good communications infrastructure – the intensification of trade and capital flows is creating a new type of regional or global concentration of specialised skills, financial services and management (such cities are often the headquarters of transnational corporations) in an environment conducive to the co-ordination of and networking among various activities. Such hub cities may also be megacities but need not be so large. There are also many smaller cities and regions that have developed some quite specialised expertise as the basis for their exports to domestic and foreign markets.

For the non-OECD economies, the combination of human needs (for employment, health, education, housing and transport) with the demands of the business community for services and infrastructure, constitute a formidable fiscal and organisational challenge for urban management. The environmental problems are also frequently enormous as pollution loadings increase without commensurate investment in environmental infrastructure; cities are frequently choked by traffic problems and suffer from huge housing and other service deficits.

Globalisation, by expanding trading opportunities, can reinforce the role of major cities within countries as "windows on the world". As export production and foreign investment generate new employment and rising incomes, there will be multiplier effects on demand for a variety of goods and services, including those that improve the quality of urban life. Also, by strengthening links between cities and exposing their populations to international influences, globalisation can facilitate the sharing of ideas and the transfer of know-how on various aspects of urban management, *e.g.*, urban transport, housing, land-use planning, environment, urban public finance and other aspects of public administration. The OECD Members have considerable experience that can be of value to non-members, including in such areas as public-private co-operation in provision of various public goods, innovations in the design and finance of urban infrastructure, market-based housing strategies, and local community involvement in the setting of priorities and the design of urban programmes. In the end, a more coherent, integrated approach to urban development will reduce the environmental and social costs associated with urban growth in the global economy.

– human capital development through investment in education and health, and the enhanced participation of all people, notably women, in economic and political life;

– adequate infrastructure for energy, transport and communications, extending to more backward areas and linking them more closely to national and international markets;

– easier access, notably for the poor, to productive assets like land and to financing *e.g.*, through encouragement of micro-investment lending institutions.

This list of measures, adapted from the 1995 DAC policy statement on *Development Partnerships in the New Global Context*, provides shape to the development co-operation agenda for helping poor countries to generate linkage-based development. It emphasises the importance of human and institutional development and of strengthened internal economic linkages to the capacity to become an active player in the global economy. The recent histories of the newly industrialising economies of Asia and to a lesser extent Latin America show that progress on each of these fronts can launch a nation into a dynamic phase of rapidly expanding linkages with the world economy. The optimistic message for all developing countries is that this process, operating over just two to three decades, can produce dramatic economic transformations.

OECD countries have much to gain through the economic strengthening of the least developed countries and regions. Although OECD governments are struggling to live within tighter budgets and development assistance programmes have been among the hardest hit by budget cuts, development assistance will continue to play an essential role in creating the conditions for integrating these countries into the global economy. In order to identify the most effective approaches, close partnership with the recipients would be required.

In Africa, the development record has been largely one of failure. The human cost of continuing along the same road would be intolerable. The continent has until now played a marginal role in globalisation. For a combination of reasons, most African countries failed to generate economic progress over the past three decades and many suffered economic catastrophe. Signs have emerged of a new awareness and determination on the part of some African leaders to pursue new approaches. Encouragingly, some African nations are enjoying a measure of success in striking contrast to their own recent past. It is important to build upon these successes in the interest of global peace, security and sustainability of the environment.

Consideration of African prospects helps to make concrete the analysis of linkages, development and poverty reduction for the region with the highest levels of aid dependence. Similar conclusions can be reached on other less advanced developing countries with weak links to the world economy. The essential message is that dynamic growth can be achieved through becoming an active participant in the new global economy, and the evidence shows that such growth does provide the highway to poverty reduction. Integrating with the world economy and accelerating human development are not separate agendas. This is the theme and the vision set out by the DAC in its 1996 Policy Declaration (see Box 3.2).

Accordingly, the OECD countries must:

– follow through with the policy agenda set out in that statement, which requires major changes of approach to aid relationships and processes;

– remain committed to the integration of the less advanced developing countries into the world economy, as time and policy attention are attracted by the more advanced and bigger players among the developing countries;

– make a more systematic effort to align the practice of aid to changes in economic strategies and policy thinking.

3.3. Meeting Food and Energy Needs

Feeding close to eight billion people

In the most populous non-OECD economies, growth in agricultural production over the past 15-20 years has comfortably exceeded population growth, enabling an improvement in overall nutrition, in both quantity and quality (albeit with disparities across regions and households), and a degree of food security. Both China and India have in the past achieved output growth with little or no expansion in cultivated area, *i.e.* through intensification. The challenge for agricultural policy makers in these and other non-OECD countries will be to create the conditions under which their farmers can generate sustainable sizeable production increases with a relatively plentiful supply of labour, but on a land base mostly fixed or subject to very small increases.

Agricultural self-sufficiency is a stated objective of many countries agricultural policies. A combination of high consumption growth, greater demand for meat, a removal of agricultural subsidies and protection, and domestic supply constraints, could lead to some strong adjustments in aggregate self-sufficiency in a variety of regions under the high growth scenario. While this may create concerns in importing regions, the level of import dependence should not be over-emphasised. First, the aggregate degree of import dependence reflects a diverse group of commodities. All importing regions could easily produce adequate basic food supplies if a major disruption in imports were to occur. For countries with limited endowments of land well-suited to agriculture, a more effective long-run food security strategy would be to boost non-food exports in order to secure adequate financing for food imports.

The economic cost of agricultural self-sufficiency policies have been widely documented. The annual costs of agricultural policies for the OECD countries alone are in the range of $300 billion annually, or 1.3-2.2 per cent of GDP (though these policies are not implemented exclusively in support of self-sufficiency). Recent estimates for Korea indicate that expenditures in support of agricultural policies accounted for 13 per cent of the total national budget in 1994. If China were to attempt to maintain food self-sufficiency (*i.e.* import penetration near the current level of 10 per cent of domestic demand), agricultural tariffs would need to be raised to 100 per cent, which would reduce its 2020 GDP level by 10 per cent. Even a halving of the food import bill in the year 2020 (relative to the unconstrained HG level) could cost as much as 4 per cent of GDP. Supply side policies would probably provide a more adequate response.

Food availability – three cases

The Chinese case. The long run prospects for agriculture in China have received more attention than most others because of the potential for large impacts on world markets. Still, while in the HG scenario China's agricultural demand would grow at almost twice the world average, by 2020 China would account for only about one-tenth of world agricultural consumption (with one-fifth of the world's population). The results of various studies suggest a qualified optimism about future agricultural growth prospects in China, the qualifications relating partly to a lack of information on some important issues and more importantly to the crucial need for strong, well-articulated policies involving land tenure regulations, pricing, agricultural services, sustainability of agricultural practices, and public and private investment. China is not unique in these respects.

In China, the large increases in output in the 1980s (agricultural output grew by some 5.7 per cent per annum 1980-91) resulted largely from special factors that cannot be relied upon in the long term. Indeed, private investment in agriculture has been very low for many years (a consequence, among other things, of institutional and legal problems of security of land tenure and a lack of farm credit) as has public sector investment in ancillary infrastructure off the farm. Major parts of China's collectively vast irrigation system – the backbone of crop agriculture in the central and southern parts of the country – suffer from irregularities in water supply, flooding, inadequate drainage, siltation of reservoirs, etc., and could be considerably improved and modernised. Of relevance in the longer term, there is promising research on designing low-cost water distribution systems that could greatly improve water use efficiency, not only in China. Other important problems concern alkalinity and salinity, particularly in areas using groundwater. Despite some improvements, most agricultural areas suffer from rather poor farm to market connections compounded by the low quality of transport vehicles. Similarly, vitally important agricultural research and farmer advisory services are rather weak and in urgent need of upgrading. Finally, farm gate prices of some crops are depressed by price control policies designed to give relief to urban consumers; the elimination of trade barriers would help to raise somewhat farm gate prices. Assuming progress in addressing these challenges, the HG agricultural growth rate of 3.3 per cent per annum appears plausible in the context of economy-wide growth of 8.0 per cent per annum.

Some crop yields in China, especially rice yields, are fairly high (though exaggerated by an under-reporting of the land area amounting to as much as 15-20 per cent according to recent OECD analysis). Productivity is low in the livestock sector (where the growth of demand is likely to be particularly rapid, along with feed grain requirements). There are most likely significant scale economies to be realised in meat production – for example, commercial scale poultry farms and piggeries. The substitution of high for low value agricultural produce is also likely to be an important part of the growth potential, again linked to the development of urban markets and the use of agricultural materials in processing industries.

Downside risks are *a*) failures in government policy; *b*) labour scarcities if employment in the non-farm sectors grows very rapidly; *c*) deterioration in soil and water conditions associated with inappropriate land use and a failure to make proper investments; and *d*) in respect of grains, a failure of research to develop the seeds needed for continuous improvement in yields. Also, with imports expected to supply a growing share of food demand, China will need to ensure an adequate port and transport infrastructure to expedite distribution.

The Indian case. In contrast to China's recent growth spurt in agriculture, which was helped by a move away from collective farming to the so-called household responsibility system of individual farms, India's progress owes little to such institutional changes, gaining, however, considerably from high rates of public investment, particularly in irrigation and agricultural research (for example in high yield varieties). On the other side of the coin, agriculture in India has been taxed both explicitly through procurement prices and export bans, and implicitly through the protection of the manufacturing sector. Reforms in the early 1990s are slowly eliminating both types of taxation, which should allow Indian farmers to reap the benefits of higher returns as well as providing them with a healthy production incentive. The key remaining policy issue facing the Indian government concerns input subsidies (principally of fertilisers and electricity). Though small initially, input subsidies have ballooned (reaching a level of about $5 billion in 1990), and consume over 80 per cent of public expenditures on agriculture. While the application of fertilisers has been an important factor in the growth of output in Indian agriculture, poor pricing policies typically generate inefficient use of inputs, as well as harmful environmental impacts. Moreover, the input subsidies have crowded out other important public expenditures such as irrigation, agricultural research, and public infrastructure. Spending on these items would likely be more beneficial in the long term for both output and the environment than a continued costly subsidisation of fertilisers.

The HG scenario results suggest a continuation of solid agricultural growth (3.5 per cent per annum), mainly generated from increases in investment and to a lesser extent fertiliser use. A partial switch would occur from food grains towards higher value added crops, as well as into livestock, though this latter effect would be somewhat lower than in other rapidly emerging economies because of consumer preferences. Likewise the impact on feed grain demand should be smaller. Though poultry consumption may rise rapidly, this has a much lower impact on feed demand since the conversion factor for poultry is only 2.5 to 1, as opposed to 7 to 1 for beef. Combined with sustained productivity growth, slower population growth and lower income elasticities of demand for food than in the past should allow India to maintain rough balance in its agricultural trade.

The Sub-Saharan African case. Despite some encouraging results for a few countries, no clear signs have yet emerged that agriculture in Africa plays the key role in the economy that is needed if the continent is to develop in a sustainable way. The HG case developed for Africa links an overall growth of 5.2 per cent per annum (equivalent to 2.7 per cent per capita) to an agricultural growth rate of about 4.3 per cent. High growth in agriculture would be needed *a*) because demands for agricultural goods will rise at a very brisk rate due to fast population growth and the low initial base of per capita consumption, while *b*) in net terms, Africa cannot afford to import more than a modest share of its food needs because it will take some time to develop a strong base in exports of non-agricultural goods, particularly manufactures (from this perspective, it will be vital that Africa does a good job in exploiting its comparative advantage in non-seasoned crops). Estimates for the 1980s show agricultural output growing at less than 2 per cent per annum, far below requirements for the HG case, although in longer term perspective (1966-89) foodcrop output grew significantly faster, at close to 3 per cent per annum.

What are the prospects of achieving a major improvement in agricultural performance in Africa? A 1995 International Food Policy Research Institute (IFPRI) study of long term potentials and prospects suggests action in three critical areas:

- "Increasing the productivity of agricultural production resources to achieve a 4 per cent rate of agricultural growth through in-depth scientific research, research on better practices for farm conditions, improved incentives, adequate attention to fertiliser supply and improved transport.

- Boosting national public investment in agriculture to 30 per cent of national budget outlay from the historical average of only 7 per cent with effective and increased domestic resource mobilisation.

- Improving the quality, stability, probity, and consistency of agricultural policy, encouraging effective rural participation in political systems, and developing a locally based process of analytical input into policy making."

Excellent though these suggestions are, they are quite far from current realities, thus posing a major challenge.

Energy: slowing demand growth and ensuring security of supplies

A conservative estimate by the IEA places cumulative investment (1994-2010) in power generation capacity in the Big Five (for a capacity increase of roughly 660 GW) at close to 500 billion 1990 dollars. Assuming a similar rate of investment from 2010 to 2020, and averaging the investment over the whole period to 2020 suggests an average investment requirement per annum equivalent to about 1 per cent of GDP (and 3-4 per cent of total investment). The IEA estimate does not include early replacement or upgrading of existing generation equipment, nor does it include the cost of flue gas desulphurisation equipment for new oil and coal capacity.

Thus, apart from mitigating the environmental impact, there is great interest in measures that would reduce energy usage and thereby lower production and investment requirements. In many countries, large prospective gains could come through energy pricing reforms and other incentives to reward conservation in energy use. A recent IEA study argues that with power tariffs only about one-half the level needed to fund capacity expansion, many non-OECD economies need major price adjustments. The pace of modernisation of technology in industry will also have a big impact. Old plants are typically far less efficient in the use of energy than any replacement, and several key non-OECD economies, such as China and Russia, have a large inheritance of obsolete technology from the era of central planning. In China, data on GDP growth and energy consumption over the past few years suggest that energy is being used more efficiently in recently commissioned plants.

Coal production and consumption are highly localised and are of major importance in China and India, where coal can be mined in large volume at a relatively low cost. Even so, to meet demand in the HG case would require sharply increased production, calling for expansion at an average annual rate of 3-4 per cent. Indonesian coal production, though relatively small, is also increasing rapidly. Output in 1995 reached 40 million tonnes (Mt), of which 32 Mt was exported, mostly at a premium reflecting its low sulphur content. A large fraction of the delivered cost of coal is accounted for by transport costs so that the expense of the additional transportation capacity must be added to the heavy expenditure on new investments in mining.

The main use of coal is in base load power generation, though other uses (principally as a heat source to fire boilers and for iron ore processing) remain important but are no longer growing at the world level. In many parts of the world, notably in the OECD, coal is giving way to gas in power generation. Technical improvements in the design, operation and efficiency of combined cycle gas turbines (see Box 3.3) have been responsible for a considerable change in the economics of power generation favouring gas over other energy sources. Quicker to build and with lower capital costs, gas-fuelled plants also emit fewer pollutants per unit of energy than other fossil fuel based plants.

One of the main constraints on the use of gas in power generation is the high cost of transport (which necessitates pipelines or specialised ships to move gas in liquid form). Only about 19 per cent of gas output is traded at the present time, though by 2020 this could rise to around 30 per cent. In total, IEA estimates that the use of natural gas might expand its share in total energy supply from 22 per cent in 1994 to some 25 per cent by 2010. Among the non-OECD economies, Russia and Indonesia are large producers and users of natural gas; other Big Five countries have little by way of domestic supplies though there exist

Box 3.3. Combined Cycle Gas Turbines:

An Example of Rapid Technological Change in Electric Power Generation

For many OECD countries and increasing numbers of non-OECD countries the Combined Cycle Gas Turbine (CCGT) has become the dominant choice for base load electricity generation. Only a decade ago gas turbines were not considered a credible competitor to coal, nuclear or hydroelectric generation. This radical change is the result of changes in technology, fuel markets and the structure of electricity markets.

Technology: gas turbines burn natural gas or clean distillates in an engine whose basic design is the same that of jet aircraft engines. Their exhaust is sufficiently hot that it may be used to raise steam for electricity production from a steam turbine. The combination of gas and steam turbine is called a combined cycle gas turbine (CCGT). Gas turbines alone and in combined cycle have been used since the 1950s, but their economics based on low capital cost and relatively high fuel costs kept them confined largely to meeting peak demand. Gas turbine technology benefited greatly during the 1980s from developments in military jet aircraft engines. This aviation market demanded lighter, more powerful, more efficient engines. These objectives were achieved by burning fuel at ever-higher temperatures. This required new materials and design concepts.

These technical advances worked equally well for gas turbines on land, delivering improved efficiency. The higher temperatures also meant that the exhaust gas was now hotter and improved the economics of adding a steam turbine to generate additional electricity from the same fuel input. Currently, CCGT plants convert 55 per cent of the energy in the fuel into electricity. Soon 60 per cent efficient plants will be in operation. The best coal power plants achieve 45-48 per cent efficiency. The CCGT plants are simpler and cheaper than coal power plants and can be built much more quickly. Capital costs of CCGTs stand at about half the cost of coal-fired plants. The cost of electricity from CCGTs can be two-thirds the price, or lower in some markets, compared to that from coal-fired plants.

Fuel markets: in the past decade gas prices, and expectations of future long-term prices, have been substantially lower than over the previous decade. Fuel price differentials between gas, nuclear and coal are now relatively less important than capital cost differentials. The natural gas infrastructure has matured, increasing the availability of gas for power generation.

Electricity market structure: increased competition in electricity supply in many countries has attracted new entrants and increased cost-consciousness. This has emphasised the advantage of CCGTs in cost of electricity and has also increased the importance of rapid construction. Government restrictions on the use of natural gas for electricity generation have been lifted in many countries, including the United States and the member states of the EU. Environmental standards have increased capital and running costs of coal power stations relative to gas-fired power stations. Likewise, stricter safety standards at nuclear plants have increased their costs relative to CCGTs.

Future developments: sweeping technological changes in base load electricity generation are very rare with perhaps only five significant technology-driven instances over the course of more than a century: the hydroelectric turbine, the steam turbine, pulverisation of coal, nuclear fission and now CCGTs.

Combined Cycle Gas Turbines are likely to dominate the market for new power plants in most of the OECD over the medium term. Yet many developing countries have large coal reserves and poor access to natural gas. Advanced clean coal technologies with efficiencies greater than 50 per cent and very low emissions of pollutants could become competitive in these markets through a combination of environmental regulatory pressure and cost reduction through further technical advances. Several renewable energy technologies have prospects of substantial technology-driven cost reductions.

Source: OECD, International Energy Agency.

possibilities of expanded trade, for example, via a link between China and the Siberian or Central Asian gas fields. In both China and India, the use of gas for power generation competes with its use as a feedstock in the production of nitrogenous fertiliser.

Crude oil is by far the major traded source of energy. The significant fraction of oil demand met through trade today is expected to increase considerably over the period to 2020, as consumption outstrips production by a wide margin in the net consuming regions. Primarily used in the transportation sector, oil can be used for base load power generation in relatively small, less capital-intensive investments. In future, high interest rates coupled with a shortage of investment capital for new power capacity could favour more use of oil for power generation from small independent power producers.

Given known reserves, supply potentials, and extraction costs, rising oil demand would not necessarily lead to rapid increases in oil (or other energy) prices in the absence of supply disruptions. Indeed, technological innovation in recent years (3-D seismic and horizontal drilling) have reduced the costs of exploration and production and stimulated production from formerly difficult fields. The IEA assumes real oil prices rise rather slowly – at roughly 2 per cent per annum – until 2010; in the HG scenarios for the period after 2010 a further rise at the rate of 1 per cent per annum is assumed; by this period new technologies may be increasing the viability of backstop non-conventional options for energy; also, at the oil prices ruling after 2010, the extraction of oil from tar sands (of which large reserves are located in several areas, *e.g.*, in Canada) would probably also be profitable. The main oil exporting Middle East countries would most likely seek to keep prices low enough to discourage investment in alternative sources such as tar sands for as long as possible. However, supply disruptions leading to sharp price rises and prolonged periods of higher prices cannot be ruled out.

The growing extent to which oil is used in transportation, for which no substitutes are readily available, suggests that a supply shock would have to have very large price effects to rebalance short run supply and demand. The energy security issue posed by the projected growing dependence on Middle East oil argues for a careful review of oil taxation and other policies in some countries so as to encourage further oil conservation and promote efficiency in its use, and for adequate consultation and co-ordination of national responses in the event of an oil supply shock. The increased oil import dependence of non-OECD countries and regions suggests an increasingly powerful shared interest with OECD Members in avoiding oil price shocks and market fluctuations. The policy of holding strategic stocks of oil (and diversification of energy sources) would be more effective if adopted not just by OECD countries but also by major importers such as China and India. Conditions for global co-ordination with respect to energy security seem likely to improve. Opening up to foreign investment in countries with major untapped oil and gas potential such as Russia could also be helpful in this respect.

3.4. Environmentally Sustainable Development

In the past 20 years OECD countries have made significant progress in tackling many of the most pressing local and regional environmental problems. In the case of urban air pollution, this has meant reductions in SO_2, total particulate matter, and lead; meanwhile, NO_2, photochemical smog and fine particulates remain problematic. As for water pollution, microbial pollution has been largely brought under control, but chemical pollution remains a serious problem. The release of certain persistent chemicals (DDT, PCBs, and mercury compounds) into the environment has been reduced but not eliminated. Recent progress in reducing noise pollution from aircraft is being offset by increased noise from land vehicles, and road congestion and associated pollution remain concerns in many large cities. Solid-waste volumes continue to rise and with them disposal problems, with growing scarcity of landfill space and strong NIMBY (not-in-my-backyard) opposition in some places to siting of incinerators. While efforts to protect natural habitats and remaining biodiversity in OECD countries have met with some success, the effects of economic development continue to place strong pressures on the natural environment.

In achieving environmental improvements to date, effective policies and institutions have been established and significant resources invested, frequently between one and two per cent of GDP. Important challenges remain for OECD countries. A number of "win-win" opportunities have been exploited and making further progress may entail more difficult trade-offs or confronting powerful lobbies. Greater attention will need to be given in policy formulation to the choice of cost-effective policy instruments, notably various economic instruments. Less than satisfactory progress has occurred in areas where effective implementation depends on significant changes or reforms in economic or sectoral policies, particularly energy (see Box 3.4), transport and agriculture. In the case of transport, for example, one study for the United States estimates that the provision of free workplace parking (a tax-free benefit-in-kind) is equivalent to a subsidy of $19 billion whose removal would reduce carbon emissions by some 19 million tonnes. Removal of other transport-related subsidies could reduce emissions by an additional 40 million tonnes.

Partly because of favourable technological developments and structural changes in their economies, some OECD countries appear to have been quite successful in "decoupling" certain types of pollution from economic growth. For example, energy intensities of GDP have declined steadily since 1974, despite significant decreases in real energy prices since 1984. The rate of improvement has stabilised however in recent years, and some of the less developed OECD countries are experiencing rising energy intensities.

Box 3.4.   Coal (and Energy) Subsidies

Coal is heavily subsidised in both OECD countries and non-OECD economies. Producer subsidy equivalents in selected OECD countries are shown in the table below, along with number of jobs remaining in coal mining. The implied subsidy per job varies widely across countries, in one case reaching more than $170 000. Available data suggests that direct subsidies for coal production in several (but not all) OECD countries have declined since the late 1980s. This does not appear to have led automatically to increased coal imports. Although coal imports to OECD Europe appear to have risen as domestic coal production has fallen, the growth in the former has been much smaller than the decline in the latter.

In Russia, subsidies to the coal industry equal an estimated 1.3 per cent of GNP and are equivalent to 144 per cent of the pithead price. Final users pay one-third of the unsubsidised price. In China, the state price for coal in the mid-1980s was approximately one-quarter the market price. Total subsidies amounted to about $2.5 billion. In India, in 1991-92, the ratio of domestic prices for coal to border prices was 0.6, reflecting in part the presence of significant subsidies.

Removal of energy subsidies would in many cases lead to substantial environmental improvements. One study estimates that worldwide energy subsidies amount to a negative carbon tax of $40 a ton and that their removal would reduce CO_2 emissions from baseline levels by 4-5 per cent.

Coal subsidies in OECD countries in 1993

	$/tonne	$ million	coal mining employment
Canada	12	48	9 000
France	43	428	...
Germany	109	6 688	174 000
Japan	161	1 034	6 000
Spain	84	856	36 000
Turkey	143	416	66 000
UK	15	873	48 000
US	0	0	...

Sources: Michaelis, L, (1996): "The Environmental Implications of Energy and Transport Subsidies" in OECD (1996), Subsidies and the Environment – Exploring the Linkages. Paris; Clarke, R. and Winters, A. (1995), "Energy Pricing for Sustainable Development" in Goldin, I. and Winters, A.(eds) The Economics of Sustainable Development. Cambridge University Press, Cambridge; OECD (1996), Industrial Structure Statistics, 1994; Shah, A. and Larsen, B. (1992), "World Energy Subsidies and Global Carbon Emissions". Background Paper prepared for the 1992 World Development Report. World Bank.

OECD Members' environmental policy agendas focus increasingly on difficult global problems like climate change as well as the management of shared natural resources; in both these areas, progress to date has been slow. The globalisation of environmental problems will inevitably lead to closer contact between OECD and non-OECD countries on environmental issues, though even on national policy concerns there is scope for co-operation as growing prosperity in a number of non-OECD countries brings in train environmental challenges similar to those currently or only recently confronting OECD Members. On the global environment, one potential source of friction in future is that while, with rapid industrial development, the non-OECD countries will make a growing contribution to global pollutants like greenhouse gases, the strongest public demands for reducing such pollutants come from OECD Member countries. On the other hand, sizeable differences across countries in the costs of measures to reduce global pollutants offer the potential for large mutual gains through an efficient global allocation of abatement activities, accompanied by appropriate financing arrangements.

Environmental challenges facing non-OECD countries

The rapid economic growth associated with the HG scenario is bound to add to environmental stresses through growing consumption of fossil fuels and associated emissions of noxious gases, rising volumes of hazardous and other wastes, more intensive agriculture, logging and fisheries exploitation, and growing demands for fresh water resources. Linkage-promoting policies and other economic reforms could mitigate some effects, *e.g.* by promoting greater cost competition and discouraging inefficient use of energy and raw material inputs, improving access to cleaner technologies, and transmitting through trade the preferences (including environmental preferences) of consumers in high income countries to producers in low income ones. In speeding the reduction of rural poverty, rapid growth in non-OECD countries should also relieve some poverty-related environmental stresses by accelerating demographic changes and the shift of population out of low-productivity employment like cultivation of marginal lands, with its associated deforestation and land degradation. Some of the main national environmental policy challenges facing non-OECD countries are briefly described here.

Urban Air Quality: the health impacts of urban air pollution and associated economic costs can be severe (Box 3.5 summarises recent pollution damage cost estimates for several Asian cities). In 1988, chronic obstructive pulmonary disease linked to exposure to fine particulates, SO_2 and other pollutants accounted for 26 per cent of all deaths in China. Indoor exposure to emissions from poor quality coal used for cooking and heating also presents a major health risk, increasing the incidence of both pulmonary disease and stroke. The economic costs are also high: for China's urban areas as a whole, the annual cost of air pollution-related deaths is estimated at about $880 million. Emissions from road transport represent some of the most important local environmental problems. Globally, the number of motor vehicles could grow from 580 million in 1990 to 816 million by 2010. The non-OECD economies likely will account for an overwhelming share of the increase. The number of vehicles in China is estimated to be growing by 14 per cent per annum. In Indonesia, the transport sector is projected to grow by 6-8 per cent per year: fuel use in transport, and its associated pollution, is projected to increase to twice the 1990 level by 2000, five times by 2010 and nine times by 2020. Road transport already accounts for 57 per cent of air pollution in New Delhi, 75 per cent in Beijing, 70 per cent in Manila and 86 per cent in Kuala Lumpur.

Water Availability (see Figure 3.7): Currently, some 28 countries with a total population of 338 million are considered water scarce (defined as less than 1 000 m³ of annual renewable water resources per person). By 2 025 the number

◆ Figure 3.7. *Annual freshwater withdrawal*[1]

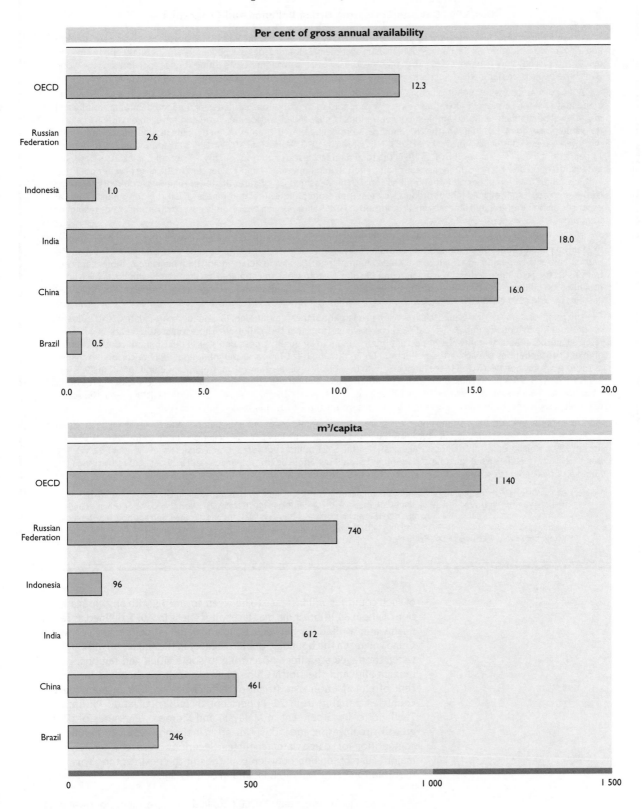

Per cent of gross annual availability

OECD	12.3
Russian Federation	2.6
Indonesia	1.0
India	18.0
China	16.0
Brazil	0.5

0.0   5.0   10.0   15.0   20.0

m³/capita

OECD	1 140
Russian Federation	740
Indonesia	96
India	612
China	461
Brazil	246

0   500   1 000   1 500

1. Data for OECD exclude the Czech Republic, Hungary, Korea, and Poland.
Source: OECD, UNEP (1997), *Global Environnement Outlook 1.*

Box 3.5. Damage Costs from Urban Pollution and Congestion

Urban pollution problems are growing more severe in many large cities of the developing world. The rapid pace of urban and industrial development in East and Southeast Asia over the past few decades has put severe strains on the urban environment. Only recently have economists begun to measure the associated economic costs. Three studies sponsored by the World Bank have applied similar methodologies to estimate damage costs in Jakarta, Bangkok, and several cities of Malaysia.

A study of air and water pollution damage in Jakarta, Indonesia (World Bank 1994a), estimates that the health effects alone may cost the economy $500 million a year. With regard to air pollution, estimates of the incremental morbidity and mortality attributable to elevated ambient concentrations of suspended particulates, lead and nitrogen dioxide had a central value (for 1990) of $220 million (the NO_2 damages were negligible). Estimates of the benefits in reduced mortality from improved water quality were in the range of $285-315 million in 1990 (World Bank 1994a). Since Jakarta accounted for around 14 per cent of Indonesia's non-oil GDP in 1990, the total damage costs amount to roughly 3.5 per cent of Jakarta's domestic product in that year – 1.5 per cent in the case of air pollution and between 1.9 and 2.1 per cent in the case of water pollution – which comes to one-half per cent of non-oil national GDP. Measured GDP figures are lower than they would otherwise be by the amount of the reduced labour productivity resulting from pollution-related illnesses. On the other hand, medical expenses on pollution-related illnesses are an addition to GDP but impose an opportunity cost by diverting scarce resources from productive uses.

The methodology developed in the Jakarta study for estimating air pollution damages (Ostros, 1992) has been applied to Malaysia and to Bangkok. In the case of Malaysia (World Banks, 1993), only two pollutants were evaluated – suspended particulates and lead. Reducing TSP levels in Kuala Lumpur, Johor, Perak and Pulau Pinang from measured ambient concentrations to the recommended Malaysian guideline (90 μ/m^3) would yield an estimated saving from health costs averted of roughly $560 million. A 90-per cent reduction in lead levels in Kuala Lumpur and Selangor (e.g., through a ban on leaded gasoline) would yield estimated savings of some $425 million in reduced health damages.

The Bangkok study (World Bank 1994b) considers a larger number of pollutants (suspended particulates, lead, SO_2 and ozone) and yields equally impressive damage cost savings from reduced pollution. The estimated benefits in terms of reduced morbidity and mortality of a 20 per cent improvement in air quality (measured as a 20 per cent reduction in average ambient concentrations of each of the pollutants) are in the range of $750 to $3 140 million (at 1989 prices and exchange rate). To get some perspective on these numbers, note that the GDP of the Bangkok metropolitan region (BMR) in 1989 was approximately $31.5 billion. Thus, if the actual health damages were at the upper end of the range, the size of the resultant economic losses amount to an extraordinary 10 per cent of 1989 BMR GDP (or 5 per cent of national GDP). Even if the actual damages were at the lower end of the range, the losses would come to 1.2 per cent of national GDP.

The same two World Bank studies have estimated the economic costs in Kuala Lumpur and Bangkok respectively of traffic congestion. The Kuala Lumpur study estimates the average time lost per passenger per day in traffic jams at 15 minutes in 1992, which works out to a total wage cost of some $427 million per year (at an average hourly wage of $2.65). The Bangkok study considers what the time and running cost savings would be of a 10 per cent and a 20 per cent reduction in the number of peak hour trips. The cost savings work out to $431 million and $813 million respectively.

Sources: Bart D. Ostro (1992), "Estimating the Health and Economic Effects of Air Pollution in Jakarta: A Preliminary Assessment", Draft Report prepared for the World Bank, Washington DC, September 18; World Bank (1993), Malaysia: Managing Costs of Urban Pollution. Country Economic Report, Washington DC, November 15; World Bank (1994a), Indonesia: Environment and Development, Washington DC; World Bank (1994b), Thailand: Mitigating Pollution and Congestion Impacts in a High-growth Economy. Country Economic Report, Washington DC, February 14.

of such countries will increase to between 46 and 52, with an aggregate population of about 3 billion. India may face water stress in 2 025, defined as renewable fresh water availability between 1 000 and 1 700 m^3 per person per year, while China will reach the boundary of this category in the same year although chronic water shortages are already occurring in some cities and regions, e.g. Beijing municipality and the North China Plain. Agriculture accounts for over 70 per cent of global water use. Irrigation efficiencies are low in many developing countries, ranging from 25-40 per cent in India, Pakistan, Philippines and Thailand to 40-45 per cent in Malaysia and Morocco. Pressures of population growth, urbanisation and industrialisation in the non-OECD economies will fuel competition for scarce water resources. Securing access to water may become a major cause of tension between countries in the next century. This is already the situation in the Middle East and in South Asia.

Water quality: every day, 25 000 people die as a result of poor water quality, with approximately 1.7 billion (almost one-third the world's population) without access to safe water. The limited reach of sanitation infrastructure is a major contributor to high rates of microbial contamination of drinking water. Waterborne diseases remain the single largest cause of human sickness and death worldwide, impacting most severely on children and the poor.

The non-OECD countries probably still enjoy more "win-win" and low-cost opportunities for confronting environmental problems than do OECD countries. The process of economic reform may create opportunities for earlier integration of environmental considerations into sectoral policies than has been the case in OECD countries. As competitive pressures intensify and income levels rise in non-OECD countries, their environmental policy agendas will probably converge towards those of OECD Members, but the process could take many years for the poorer countries.

Environmental policies in non-OECD economies will need to evolve to reflect growing economic maturity and changing public preferences, and OECD experience can be valuable as non-OECD countries seek to strengthen their environmental management systems. In general, these systems are shaped by a variety of factors such as underlying environmental conditions, the intensity and structure of economic activity and the extent of public environmental awareness and pressure. Thus environmental priorities will not be uniform because different national circumstances will lead to placing different values on environmental protection; nevertheless, the deeper the process of linkage-intensive development, the greater the mutual benefit in developing common perspectives on environmental problems. Shared interests are likely in policies that enhance economic efficiency, such as through dematerialisation and decoupling economic development from resource/energy consumption, integrating economic and environmental policies, and promoting the use of cleaner technologies. Many non-OECD economies have an interest in the experience of OECD countries in applying the Polluter-Pays-Principle and establishing the policy and institutional framework for effective environmental management, including the financing of priority environmental projects. Equally, both groups of countries have a shared interest in methods for prioritising problems, applying cost-effective approaches and instruments, and minimising the economic and financial impacts of environmental policies.

An exercise in co-operation on environmental policy and institution building involving the OECD and the countries of Central and Eastern Europe has demonstrated that co-operative programmes can be designed to address both the national priorities of recipient countries as well as regional and global concerns. Other guiding principles for co-operation emerging from the Central and Eastern European experience are the following: *a*) base environmental priorities on a careful comparison of costs and benefits; *b*) implement policies and invest in projects which provide both economic and environmental benefits; *c*) harness market forces for pollution control wherever possible; *d*) concentrate on local problems first; *e*) set standards that are realistic and enforceable; *f*) involve local people in setting priorities and in implementing solutions; *g*) clarify responsibility for past environmental damage.

Globalisation may lead to increased conflicts between the two groups of countries. While trade and investment per se do not generate environmental problems, they do amplify market and policy failures inadequately addressed by environmental policies. The intensification of environmental pressures by increased trade may thus generate opposition to trade liberalisation. Further, governments have at times used trade policies (*e.g.*, bans on imports) as an instrument to protect national and global environmental resources, giving rise to trade disputes. Trade instruments have also been used in the context of certain multilateral environmental agreements (MEAs) – in the case of the Montreal Protocol, to encourage accession; in the case of CITES (Convention on International Trade in Endangered Species), to constrain demand. Some such uses of trade instruments remain controversial and discussions are underway within the WTO to develop guidelines on when they might be used for environmental purposes. Market access requirements are another potential source of tension. Thus, eco-labelling and packaging rules might function as non-tariff trade barriers in the guise of environmental standards. The continuing use of subsidies – for example in agriculture and energy – in both OECD countries and non-OECD economies distorts resource allocation, while it can damage the environment at the same time. The environmental distributional impacts of closer OECD-NME linkages may fuel conflicts about the geographical location of polluting industries, the relative share of total non-renewable resource consumption, and the export of hazardous wastes and substances.

Spurred by intensified competition, governments in both OECD countries and the non-OECD economies will come under increasing pressure to minimise cost and competitiveness impacts of environmental regulations on domestic producers. This has led some commentators to fear a "race to the bottom" in environmental standards and policy (or policy inertia as governments may only be willing to introduce tighter regulations in concert with their major competitors). Thus far, empirical work does not provide strong grounds for this fear. While historically many countries have followed a strategy of "grow now and clean up later", there is now growing recognition of the associated ecological and economic costs, as well as a greater appreciation of the role of sustainable development policies that integrate economic and environmental goals. Also, some have argued that an early strengthening of regulations can bring first-mover advantages in the form of new technologies that later followers would eventually need.

Policies for the global environment

In an era when environmental problems are increasingly supra-national, the limited capacity of existing international institutions to respond to these challenges is becoming more visible and acute. In response to the new global problems, the framework for international environmental governance has been evolving and both institutions and law have quickly developed to cover a broad range of areas. However, considerable diversity and a measure of incoherence is also reflected in the wide variety of institutional and legal responses and this is coupled with limited power to enforce international commitments. Global co-operation will need to be based on acceptance of the principle of "common but differentiated responsibilities": this principle states that countries share a common responsibility to protect international environmental resources, but do not share equally the responsibility for addressing the problems. Historically, industrialised countries have borne a greater responsibility for pollution of the global commons and consumption of natural resources. Moreover, in most cases they have a greater financial and technical capacity to pursue global environmental objectives.

The major challenge is to reach agreement on the practical application of the principle. Various approaches have been tried or proposed to give effect to the principle of common but differentiated responsibility; many involve multilateral environmental agreements (MEAs):

Compensatory financing: a number of MEAs disburse funds which usually are provided by OECD countries. For example, the fund established under the Montreal Protocol had approved $214 million for 461 projects by May 1996. Yet, India alone could require an estimated $2 billion to phase out all ozone-depleting substances. Under the Framework Convention on Climate Change, by one estimate, $480 billion would be required to meet the Toronto Conference target of 20 per cent reduction in CO_2 emissions by 2005. The Global Environment Facility, established after Rio, has provided financial support for projects on climate change, bio-diversity, international waters, and phase-out of ozone depleting substances. By July 1996, 59 projects had been approved, representing $506 million.

Preferential technology transfer: provisions for such transfers exist in the Basel Convention and Montreal Protocol. Under the latter, some CFC-free technologies have been put in the public domain through industry coalitions (*e.g.* representing major electronics companies) but commercial considerations often impede rapid and broad diffusion.

Differentiated obligations: some MEAs establish differentiated compliance schedules for implementing agreed actions. This is the case, for example, with the Montreal Protocol, where developing country signatories enjoy a 10-year grace period.

Joint Implementation: under the FCCC, the concept of Joint Implementation (JI) involves agreed reduction commitments of one country being attained through the realisation of abatement in another country at a lower cost. As of July 1996 under the Activities Implemented Jointly (AIJ) pilot phase (whereby joint activities are entered but no crediting is allowed), 32 projects had received official bilateral approval, mostly in CEECs and Russia. A variety of difficult issues need resolution before such a system is institutionalised: determining baseline emissions, crediting avoided emissions, and monitoring performance. In addition, AIJ has been criticised for potentially providing a substitute for ODA and for reducing incentives in OECD countries to reduce CO_2 emissions at home or to seek technological breakthroughs.

Tradeable permits: a system of tradeable permits would involve establishing a market in abatement obligations. Various studies have demonstrated that, in principle, significant emission reductions could be achieved much more efficiently than with a strict system of equivalent national reductions. However, the establishment of such a system would have to overcome a variety of technical and political problems associated with the initial target-setting and permit allocation and with system administration.

Environmental taxes: environmental taxes have been proposed, most often carbon/energy taxes, with the aim of achieving environmental objectives at least social cost, though a perception of uneven distribution of costs often gives rise to political resistance. Some proposals call for the establishment of an international body to collect and redistribute revenues. A reluctance to create an international revenue-raising authority has also impeded developments of this type.

Strengthening environmental institutions

Numerous proposals have been advanced over the years to redefine and strengthen the roles of international environmental institutions, and also to strengthen the environmental performance of multilateral economic and development bodies. In recent years, some progress has been made in "greening" international institutions. As of July 1996, the World Bank was financing 153 environmental projects in 62 countries, amounting to $11.5 billion in loans. The European Bank for Reconstruction and Development includes environment as a guiding principle in its founding charter.

It is beyond the scope of this study to analyse the existing system of international environmental law and institutions. Nevertheless, among the objectives that a redesigned international institutional framework might seek to achieve are the following:

- further institutionalise sustainable development as the guiding principle for international environmental management;
- seek agreement to remove subsidies with major negative repercussions on the environment, notably in the energy, transport and agriculture areas;

- study the scope for integrating environmental considerations more fully into existing – and emerging – regional or international economic arrangements, such as the WTO, NAFTA, AFTA, Mercosur and the Multilateral Agreement on Investment;

- build consensus among stakeholders to reinforce mechanisms for international co-operation and, as appropriate, the development of binding legal instruments. In this respect, the urgency and economic costs of environmental problems, and the costs of non-action or "business as usual", need to be more strongly emphasized to decision-makers and the public;

- make negotiations of agreements more transparent, participatory and predictable *vis-à-vis* business, NGOs and public interest groups, while retaining the primacy of governments as contracting parties;

- strengthen implementation and compliance measures associated with international environmental agreements, including better co-ordination of the financial and technical co-operation provisions of different conventions;

- give more weight to the role of the private sector in the improvement of environmental performance, including both firms as leaders in the design and application of environmentally friendly technology and consumers in their role of signalling environmental values to producers;

- implement the principle of "common but differentiated" responsibilities more effectively in national environmental policies and in international agreements and

- strengthen informal and formal arrangements for dispute resolution, including the use of mediation.

The OECD has a vital role to play in improving understanding of the relationship between globalisation and the environment, in studying and sharing experience with environmental and other policies that ensure consistency between economic and environmental objectives, and in fostering dialogue and co-operation with non-OECD countries. The principal elements of OECD's outreach work in relation to sustainable development policies could include: *i*) a more structured policy dialogue with some of the major non-OECD economies, focusing first on their national environmental priorities but creating the confidence required to start addressing the more difficult, shared environmental challenges; *ii*) strengthening analytical work to support this dialogue and joint reflection, including quantitative analysis and scenario development to deepen understanding of the environmental implications of globalisation and linkages; *iii*) deepening work on trade-investment-environment linkages – *e.g.*, exploring the scope for integrating environmental considerations into investment regimes like MAI, monitoring the trade and competitiveness impacts of environmental policies, and promoting the re-orientation of environmentally damaging subsidy programmes, particularly in the agriculture and energy sectors; *iv*) examining specific mechanisms for reducing the barriers to the adoption and diffusion of cleaner technologies, particularly in the major non-OECD economies; *v*) engaging in a dialogue key stakeholders in the globalisation process, such as business, trade unions, environmental citizens organisations, the financial and insurance sectors and consumers; and *vi*) strengthening co-operation with donors, development banks and others working with the non-OECD economies, drawing on OECD's accumulated experience and networks in environmental management co-operation in Central and Eastern Europe, the NIS, China, India, Vietnam and the Dynamic Non-OECD Economies of Asia and Latin America.

NOTES ON THE SOURCES

Chapter 1

This study is a sequel to the first Linkages study, OECD (1995), *Linkages: OECD and Major Developing Economies*, Paris, which noted the growing importance to the OECD economies of trade, investment and other links to certain major developing economies, notably China.

Around the same time as the publication of the first OECD Linkages Study, the World Bank's 1995 *Global Economic Prospects and the Developing Countries* contained a chapter on what it dubbed "reverse linkages", *i.e.*, growing economic impacts from developing countries to developed ones as a result of trade, investment and growth trends. More recently, the 1997 *World Economic Outlook* of the IMF is devoted to the challenges and opportunities of globalisation for both developed and developing countries and the World Bank's 1997 *Global Economic Prospects* takes a long-term forward look at the world economy (to 2020) and, more specifically, at the evolving place therein of the same Big Five countries studied here (Brazil, China, India, Indonesia and Russia).

On long term growth of the world economy, the authoritative work is: Maddison, Angus (1995), *Monitoring the World Economy* 1820-1992, OECD Development Centre Study, Paris.

On recent global trade trends, references include: Inter-American Development Bank (1996), *Integration and Trade in the America*, Washington DC.; OECD (1996), *The Economic Outlook*, Paris; WTO (1996), *The Trade Report and Trade and Foreign Direct Investment*, Geneva. United Nations (1996), *World Economic and Social Survey*, New York; UNCTAD (1996), *The Trade and Development Report*, Geneva; "Recent trends in foreign direct investment" chapter in *Financial Market Trends* Nrs. 64, OECD (June 1996) and 67 (June 1997); *World Investment Report 1997*, UNCTAD (1997); *International direct investment statistics Year-book* 1997; OECD (forthcoming). SACHS, J. and A. WARNER (1995), "Economic reform and the process of global integration", Brookings Papers on Economic Activity, Vol. 1.

On global trade policy, major references include: Bergsten, Fred (1996), "Globalizing Free Trade", *Foreign Affairs*; "Global Trade Policy", Special Issue, The *World Economy*, 1996; Goldin, I. and D. van der Mensbrugghe (1992), "Trade liberalisation: what's at stake?", OECD *Development Centre Policy Brief*, No. 5, OECD, Paris; OECD (1996), *International Trade in Professional Services: Assessing Barriers and Encouraging Reform*, OECD Documents, Paris; Sauvé, Pierre (1995), "Assessing the GATS – Half-full or Half-empty?", Journal of World Trade; OECD (1995), *The New World Trading System*, Paris.

On trade in services, including scope for outsourcing: Apte, Uday (1994), "Global Disaggregation of Services; Growth Engine for the Less Developed Countries?", International Economics Department, World Bank, mimeo, Washington DC.; *International trade in professional services; advancing liberalisation through regulatory reform*, OECD Proceedings, 1997.

On recent global capital market trends, references include: Bank for International Settlements (1996), *66th Annual Report*, Berne. IMF (1996),

International Capital Markets Outlook. World Bank (1997), *Global Development Finance*, Volume 1 and 2; World Bank (1996), *World Debt Tables*. IFC (1996), *The Emerging Markets Factbook*; UNCTAD (1996), *The World Investment Report*. Baring Securities (1995), *A Fifth Wave of Global Money*, London; OECD (1995), *DAC Development Co-operation Report*; OECD (various years), *Financial Market Trends*; OECD (1996), *Statistical Yearbook on Foreign Direct Investment*, Paris; OECD (1995b), *Future Global Capital Shortages: Real Threat or Pure Fiction?*, Paris.

On taxation, "Model Tax Convention on Income and on Capital", Loose-leaf version, OECD (1997); "Transfer Pricing Guidelines for Multinational Enterprises and Tax Administrations", Loose-leaf version, OECD (1997); "Combating Bribery of Foreign Public Officials in International Transactions: the Rule of Taxation", OECD (1996); "Controlled Foreign Company Legislation, Studies in Taxation of Foreign Source Income", OECD (1996); and "Taxation and Foreign Direct Investment, The Experience of the Economies in Transition", OECD (1995).

On international pension investment, major references include: De Gregorio, Jose and P. Guidotti (1995), "Financial Development and Economic Growth", *World Development*, Vol. 23, No. 3; Fischer, Bernhard and Helmut Reisen (1994), "Pension Fund Investment: From Ageing to Emerging Markets", OECD Development *Centre Policy Brief*, No. 9, OECD, Paris; Reisen, Helmut (1997), "Liberalising Foreign Investments by Pension Funds: Positive and Normative Aspects", OECD *Development Centre Technical Papers*, No. 120, OECD, Paris.

On foreign investment and technology spillovers: Blomström, Magnus (1989), *Foreign Investment and Spillovers*, Routledge, London. "Trade and investment; transplants", OECD (1996).

On the globalisation and small and medium scale enterprises, see OECD (1997), *Globalisation and Small and Medium Enterprises* (SMEs), Vol. 2: Country Studies, Paris.

Chapter 2

On the growth experience and productivity performance of the OECD economies, major sources include: Baumol, W., R.R. Nelson and E.N. Wolff (eds.) (1994), *Convergence of Productivity: Cross-National Studies and Historical Evidence*, Oxford University Press, New York; Bayoumi, T., D. Coe and E. Helpman (1996), "R&D spillovers and global growth", CEPR *Discussion Paper* No. 1467, August; Coe, D. and E. Helpman (1995), "International R&D spillovers", *European Economic Review*, Vol. 39; Englander, A.S. and A. Gurney (1994), "Medium-term determinants of OECD productivity", OECD *Economic Studies*, No. 22, Spring; Krugman, Paul (1994), *The Age of Diminished Expectations*, Revised Edition, MIT Press, Cambridge, MA. Also, Robert J. Gordon (1996), "Problems in the Measurement and Performance of Service-Sector Productivity in the United States", NBER Working Paper 5519 (March). "Migration and Labour Market in Asia, Prospects to the Year 2000", OECD (1996). OECD (1988) *Why Economic Policies Change Course*, Paris; OECD (1992), Purchasing power parities and real expenditures, Paris. OECD (1994), "The EC's internal market: implementation and economic effects", OECD *Economic Studies* No. 23, Winter; OECD (1994), *The OECD Jobs Study*, Paris; OECD (1996), "Macroeconomic Policies and Structural Reform", Paris. Orr, A., M. Edey and M. Kennedy (1995), "Real long-term interest rates: the evidence from pooled-time-series. OECD *Economic Studies*, No. 25.

On the macroeconomic effects of ageing: Masson, P.R. and R.W. Tyron (1990), "Macroeconomic effects of projected population ageing", IMF *Working Paper*, WP/90/5, January, Washington DC.; OECD (1996), "Ageing in OECD countries: a critical policy challenge", *Social Policy Studies* No. 20, Paris.

On the growth experience and prospects in the non-OECD economies, major references include: Lucas, Robert E., Jr. (1988), "On the Mechanics of Economic Development", *Journal of Monetary Economics*, 22(1):3-42; Barro, Robert J., and Jong-Wha Lee (1994), "International Comparisons of Educational Attainment", *Journal of Monetary Economics* 32(3):363-94; Berthélemy, J.C., S. Dessus and A. Varoudakis (1997), "Human capital, trade openness and growth", OECD Development Centre, Technical Papers No. 121, January; Krugman, Paul (1994), "The Myth of Asia's Miracle", *Foreign Affairs*,73 (6):62-78. Bosworth, B., S.M. Collins and Y.C. Chen (1995), "Accounting for differences in economic growth, *Brookings Discussion Papers in International Economics* No. 115, October; Collins, Susan M. and Barry P. Bosworth (1996), "Economic Growth in East Asia: Accumulation versus Assimilation", *Brookings Papers on Economic Activity*, 2:135-203; Rodrik, Dani (1997), "TFPG Controversies, Institutions, and Economic Performance in East Asia", NBER Working Paper 5914 (February); PAGE, J. (1994), "The East Asian miracle: four lessons for development policy", in NBER *Macroeconomics Annual*, S. Fischer and J.J. Rotemberg (eds.), MIT Press, Cambridge, Mass; PETRI, P.A. (1993), *The Lessons of East Asia: Common Foundations of East Asian Success*, World Bank; STIGLITZ, J.E. (1996), "Some lessons from the East Asian miracle", *The World Bank Research Observer*, Vol. 11, No. 2, August, pp. 151-77; WORLD BANK (1993), *The East Asian Miracle*, Oxford University Press.

On trade modeling and scenario analysis: see the technical notes on the two CGE models used for this study: OECD (1997), "The Linkage Model: A Technical Note", Development Centre, mimeo, 30 May; OECD (1997), "The WorldScan Model: Background and Simulations for Linkages II", Development Centre, mimeo, 24 June. For other related modeling work, see Central Planning Bureau, Netherlands (1992), *Scanning the Future: A Long-Term Scenario Study of the World Economy* 1990-2015, The Hague. Hertel, Tom W., editor (1997), *Global Trade Analysis: Modeling and Applications*, Cambridge University Press, New York.

On agricultural prospects, principal references consulted include: Alexandratos, Nikos editor (1996), *World Agriculture Towards* 2010: an FAO Study, John Wiley, New York, NY; Bhalla, G.S. and Peter Hazell (1996), "Prospects for Balancing Food Needs with Sustainable Resources Management in India to 2020", mimeo, International Food Policy Research Institute, May; International Food Policy Research Institute (IFPRI) (1995), A 2020 *Vision for Food, Agriculture, and the Environment: The Vision, Challenge, and Recommended Action*, Washington DC.; Islam, Nurul (ed.) (1995), *Population and Food in the Early Twenty-First Century: Meeting Future Food Demand of an Increasing Population*, IFPRI, Washington DC.. Martin, Will, and Devashish Mitra (1996), "Productivity Growth in Agriculture and Manufacturing", mimeo, The World Bank, Washington DC.; OECD (1995), *Technological Change and Structural Adjustment in OECD Agriculture*, OECD, Paris; Rosegrant, Mark W., Mercedita Agcaoili-Sombilla, and Nicostrato D. Perez (1995), "Global Food Projections to 2020: Implications for Investment", IFPRI *Food, Agriculture, and the Environment Discussion Paper* 5, Washington DC.; Rosegrant, Mark W. and Robert E. Evenson (1995), "Total Factor Productivity and Sources of Long-Term Growth in Indian Agriculture", IFPRI *Environment and Production Technology Division Discussion Paper* No. 7, April, Washington DC.; OECD (1997) "Adjustment In OECD Agriculture: Issues And Policy Responses, Paris, and OECD, Agricultural Policies, Markets and Trade", in: OECD Countries: Monitoring and Evaluation 1997; "Costs and Benefits of Food Safety Regulations: Fresh Meat Hygiene Standards in the European Union",OECD (1997). "The OECD Agricultural Outlook",OECD (1995, 1996, 1997). "Implications of the Mercosur Agreement For The Grain, Animal Feed and Sugar Cane Markets", OECD (1997). "OECD Workshop on the sustainable Management of Water, in Agriculture: Issues And Policies", OECD (1997). "Regulatory Reform and the Agro-Food Sector", OECD (1996). Lawrence, R. Z. (1996) "Towards Globally Contestable Markets", *in Market Access after the Uruguay Round*

Investment, Competition and Technology Perspectives; Hartwig Dehaen, Nikos Alexandratos and Jelle Bruisma, (1997) "Prospects for The World Food Situation at the Threshold to the 21st Century", OECD 1997; Dennis R. Henderson (1997) "Between the Farm Gate and the Dinner Plate: Motivations for Industrial Change in the Processed Food Sector", OECD 1997. Alan D. Gordon (1997), "The Influence of Demographic and Lifestyle Forces on Food and Drink Consumption, and some Future Implications for Food Service, Catering and Retailing", OECD, 1997. Per Pinstrup-Andersen and Rajul Pandya-Lorch (1997), "Major Uncertainties and Risks Affecting long-term Food Supply and Demand", OECD 1997. Guy Paillotin (1997), "L'impact des biotechnologies dans le secteur de l'agro-alimentaire", OCDE 1997; Gérard Viatte and Josef Schmidhuber (1997), "Long-Term Policy Issues and Challenges for Agro-Food", OECD 1997.

On nuclear energy, "Projected Costs of Generating Electricity 1992: Update", OECD (1993). "Decommissioning of Nuclear Facilities: An Analysis of the Variability of Decommissioning Cost Estimates", OECD (1991). "Future Financial Liabilities of Nuclear Activities", OECD (1996). "The Cost of High Level Waste Disposal in Geological Repositories: An Analysis of Factors Affecting Cost Estimates", OECD (1993). "Environmental and Ethnical Aspects of Long-lived Radioactive Waste Disposal", OECD (1994). "Uranium Resources, Production and Demand", OECD/NEA (1995). "Economics of the Nuclear Fuel Cycle", OECD/NEA (1994).

On the analysis of energy prospects, greenhouse gas emissions and climate change, major references include: Asian Development Bank (ADB) (1991), *Environment Considerations in Energy Development*, Manila; Cline, William R. (1992), *The Economics of Global Warming*, Institute for International Economics, Washington DC.; Dean, Andrew, and Peter Hoeller (1992), "Costs of Reducing CO_2 Emissions: Evidence from Six Global Models", *Economics Department Working Paper* No. 122, Paris; EMF 14 (1995), "Second Round Study Design for EMF 14: Integrated Assessment of Climate Change", mimeo, *Energy Modeling Forum*, Stanford University, Stanford, CA; European Commission (EC) (1996), "European Energy to 2020: A Scenario Approach", *in Energy in Europe, Special Issue*, Spring. IEA (various years), *World Energy Outlook*, Paris. IEA/OECD (1991), *Energy Efficiency and the Environment*, Energy and the Environment Series. IEA/OECD (1994), *The Economics of Climate Change*: Proceedings of a Conference, Paris; Lee, Hiro, Joaquim Oliveira-Martins, and Dominique van der Mensbrugghe (1994), "The OECD GREEN Model: An Updated Overview", OECD *Development Centre Technical Papers*, No. 97, OECD, Paris; OECD (1992), OECD *Economic Studies: The Economic Costs of Reducing CO_2 Emissions*, No. 19, Winter 1992, OECD, Paris. OECD (1995), *Global Warming: Economic Dimensions and Policy Responses*, Paris; IEA/OECD (1994): *Development and Deployment of Technologies to Respond to Global Climate Change Concerns. Conference Proceedings*; IEA/OECD High Level Meeting, 21-22 November 1994, Paris. OECD (1997): *Climate Change: Mobilising Global Effort*, Paris; OECD (1997): International Greenhouse Gas Emission Trading. OECD Working Papers. Available at http://www.oecd.org/env/cc/toaixg.htm. OECD (1997): Lessons from Existing Systems for International Greenhouse Gas Emission Trading. OECD Working Papers. Available at http://www.oecd.org/env/cc/toaixg.htm.

Chapter 3

On regulatory reform, the major reference is: OECD (1997), *The OECD Report on Regulatory Reform*, Paris.

On OECD employment problems and the social agenda, see OECD (1994), *The OECD Jobs Study*, and subsequent documents on implementation of the recommendations in that study; also, OECD (1997), *Societal Cohesion and the Globalising Economy: What Does the Future Hold?* Paris. Peter Scherer, "Socio-economic

Change and Social Policy" in Family, Market and Community: Equity and Efficiency in Social Policy, Social Policy Studies No. 21, OECD 1997. "Trends in International Migration", 1996 Annual Report, OECD (1997).

On ageing and related issues: OECD (1995), *The Transition from Work to Retirement*, OECD Social Policy Studies, No. 16, Paris. OECD (1996), *Ageing in OECD Countries: A Critical Policy Challenge, Social Policy Studies*, No. 20, Paris.

On educational policy: OECD (1996), *Lifelong Learning for All*. Meeting of the Education Committee at Ministerial Level, 16-17 January 1996, Paris.

On social security reform: Don, Henk, and Paul Besseling (1996), "Social security reforms: why and how?" CPB *Report*, 4, Quarterly Review of CPB Netherlands Bureau of Economic Policy Analysis, pp.13-16. Leibfritz, Willi, Deborah Roseveare, Douglas Fore and Eckhard Wurzel (1996), "Ageing Populations, Pension Systems and Government Budgets – How Do They Affect Savings?" *in Future Global Capital Shortages: Real Threat or Pure Fiction?*, OECD, Paris.

On health care reform: OECD (1992), The Reform of Health Care: A Comparative Analysis of Seven OECD Countries, Health Policy Studies Series No. 2, Paris. OECD (1994), The Reform of Health Care Systems: A Review of Seventeen OECD Countries, Health Policy Studies Series No. 5, Paris.

Recent overviews of reforms in non-OECD countries and their impacts include: Sachs, J. and A. Warner (1995), "Economic reform and the process of global integration", *Brookings Papers on Economic Activity*, Vol. 1. Haggard, Stephan (1995), *Developing Nations and the Politics of Global Integration*, Brookings Institution, Washington DC.. Rodrik, Dani (1996), "Understanding Economic Policy Reform", *Journal of Economic Literature*, Vol. XXXIV, March, pp.9-41.

On trade policy reform: Judith M. Dean, Seema Desai and James Riedel (1994), "Trade Policy Reform in Developing Countries since 1985: A Review of the Evidence", World Bank Discussion Paper No. 267, Washington DC.. Constantine Michalopoulos and David Tarr (1996), Trade Performance and Policy in the New Independent States, Directions in Development Series, The World Bank, Washington DC.. Will Martin and L. Alan Winters (1995), The Uruguay Round and the Developing Economies, World Bank Discussion Paper No. 307 is a useful compilation of essays on the implications of the Uruguay Round for the developing world.

On privatisation and state enterprise reform in developing economies, see Olivier Bouin and Charles-Albert Michalet (1991), *Rebalancing the Public and Private Sectors: Developing Country Experience*, OECD Development Centre Study, Paris.

On gender issues, written contributions have been made by Patricia Alexander, Canadian Consultant to the OECD for this study; see also World Bank (1995), *Towards Gender Equality: The Role of Public Policy*, Development in Practice Series, Washington DC.. Joekes, S. (1995), *Trade-related employment for women in industry and services in developing countries*, No. 5, Occasional Paper Series, Fourth World Conference on Women, UNRISD, Geneva. UNIDO (1996), *Women in Manufacturing: Patterns, determinants and future trends*, Integration of Women in Development Unit, Vienna. "Women in the City: Housing, Services and the Urban Environment", OECD (1995).

On China. OECD (1996), *China in the 21st Century: Long-term Global Implications*; on financial sector reforms. Hassanali Mehran and Marc Quintyn (1996), "Financial Sector Reforms in China", Finance and Development, Vol. 33, No.1, March. World Bank (1995), *China: Investment Strategies for China's Coal and Electricity Delivery Systems*, 8 March 1995. World Bank (1996), *The Chinese Economy: Fighting*

Inflation, Deepening Reforms, A World Bank Country Study. Wold Bank (1996), The Chinese Economy: Fighting Inflation, Deepening Reforms. **On India**: India: Country Economic Memorandum. Five Years of Stabilization and Reform: The Challenges Ahead, World Bank, August 1996. **On Russia**: OECD (1995), OECD Economic Surveys: The Russian Federation 1995, Paris. Russian Federation: Toward Medium-Term Viability, A World Bank Country Study, 1996. **On Indonesia**: Hal Hill (1996), The Indonesian Economy since 1966, Cambridge University Press, Cambridge. Indonesia: Dimensions of Growth, World Bank, May 1996.

On Latin America: Shahid Javed Burki and Sebastian Edwards (1996), Latin America after Mexico: Quickening the Pace, World Bank Latin American and Caribbean Studies: Viewpoints, Washington DC.. Shahid Javed Burki and Sebastian Edwards (1996), Dismantling the Populist State: The Unfinished Revolution in Latin America and the Caribbean, World Bank Latin American and Caribbean Studies: Viewpoints, Washington DC..

On Sub-Saharan Africa: Jean-Claude Berthélemy, ed. (1995), Whither African Economies?, OECD Development Centre Seminars. World Bank (1995), A Continent in Transition: Sub-Saharan Africa in the Mid-1990s, Africa Region, November. For the pairwise comparisons of African and Asian countries, Peter Harrold, Malathi Jayawickrama, and Deepak Bhattasali (1996), Practical Lessons for Africa from East Asia in Industrial and Trade Policies, World Bank Discussion Paper No. 310, Washington DC..

On development co-operation, the following are the main references: CILSS/Club du Sahel (1994), "Preparing for the Future: A Vision of West Africa in the Year 2020", December, OECD, Paris. Development Co-operation Committee, OECD (1996), Shaping the 21st Century: the Contribution of Development Co-operation, Paris. Rasheed, Sadig (1996), "A New Africa in the 21st Century – What Agenda, What Conditions?" Centre for Development Policy Management, Maastricht. Report of the African Governors of the World Bank Group (1996), "Partnership for Capacity-Building in Africa. Strategies and Programme of Action", Washington DC.. Rudner, Martin (1994), Malaysian Development: A Retrospective, Carleton University Press, Ottawa. "Migration and Development, New Partnerships for Co-operation", OECD (1994). "Migration, Free Trade and Regional Integration in Central and Eastern Europe", OECD, WIFO (1997).

On globalisation and the environment, see OECD (1997), Globalisation and Environment: Preliminary Perspectives, OECD Proceedings, Paris; OECD (1997), Economic Globalisation and the Environment, Paris; also, OECD (1996), The Global Environmental Goods and Services Industry, Paris. OECD (1994): The Environmental Effects of Trade, Paris. OECD (1994): Trade and Environment: Processes and Production Methods, OECD Documents Series, Paris. OECD (1995): Report on Trade and Environment to the OECD Council at Ministerial Level. General Distribution Document OCDE/GD(95)63, Paris.

On environmental policy in OECD countries, see OECD (1996), Integrating Environment and Economy: Progress in the 1990s, Paris; also, OECD (1997), Reforming Environmental Regulation in OECD Countries, Paris; OECD (1997), Sustainable Development: OECD Policy Approaches for the 21st Century, Paris. OECD (1996): Innovative Policies for Sustainable Urban Development. The Ecological City, Paris. OECD (1995): Technologies for Cleaner Production and Products. Towards Technological Transformation for Sustainable Development, Paris. OECD (1996): Subsidies and Environment: Exploring the Linkages. OECD Documents Series, Paris. OECD (1996): Environmental Performance in OECD Countries. Progress in the 1990s, Paris. OECD (1996): Integrating Environment and Economy. Progress in the 1990s, Paris. OECD (1997): Sustainable Consumption and Production, Paris. OECD (1997b): Sustainable Consumption and Production. Clarifying the Concepts. OECD Proceedings Series, Paris. OECD (1997): Reforming Environmental Regulation in OECD Countries, Paris. OECD

(1997): OECD *Environmental Data Compendium 1997*, Paris. OECD (1997): *Sustainable Development. Special Edition of the OECD Observer* (July 1997), Paris XX. OECD (1997): *Reforming Energy and Transport Subsidies: Environmental and Economic Implications*, Paris. OECD (forthcoming): *Applying Market-based Instruments to Environmental Policies in China and OECD Countries*, Paris. OECD (forthcoming): *Cleaner Production and Waste Minimisation in OECD and Dynamic Non-OECD Economies*. OECD *Proceedings Series, Paris.*

On environmental policy in non-OECD countries, see O'Connor, David (1994), *Managing the Environment with Rapid Industrialisation: Lessons from the East Asian Experience*, OECD Development Centre Study, Paris; OECD (1994), *Applying Economic Instruments to Environmental Policies in OECD and Dynamic Non-OECD Economies*, OECD Documents, Paris; World Bank (1994), *Indonesia: Environment and Development*. World Bank Country Study, Washington DC.. OECD (1995): *Promoting Cleaner Production in Developing Countries. The Role of Development Co-operation*. OECD Documents Series, Paris. European Commission/OECD/World Bank (1994): *Environmental Action Programme for Central and Eastern Europe.*

On natural resources and the global environment, the following are principal references: Engleman, R. and LeRoy, P. (1993), *Sustaining Water. Population and the Future of Renewable Water Supplies*, Population Action International, Washington D.C; FAO (1995), *The State of World Fisheries and Aquaculture*. Rome; Flavin, C. (1997), "The Legacy of Rio" in *State of the World 1997*, Worldwatch Institute, W.W. Norton and Co. New York; French, H.F. (1997), "Learning from the Ozone Experience" in *State of the World 1997, op.cit.*; Government of Japan (1996), "A Long Term Perspective on Environment and Development in the Asia-Pacific Region", Draft Final Report on Eco Asia Long Term Perspective Project, and Report of the Third International Workshop. May 1996. Environment Agency, Government of Japan; Tokyo; Gujja, Biksham and Andrea Finger-Stich (1996), "What Price Prawn? Shrimp Aquaculture's Impact in Asia", *Environment*, 38(7), September; Pearce, D. and Warford, J. (1993), *World Without End*, Johns Hopkins University Press, Baltimore; Rosegrant, Mark W., Renato Gazmuri Schleyer, and Satya N. Yadav (1995), "Water policy for efficient agricultural diversification: market-based approaches", *Food Policy*, 20(3):203-233; Rosegrant, Mark W. and Robert Livernash (1996), "Growing More Food, Doing Less Damage", *Environment*, 38(7), September; UNEP (1997), *Global Environment Outlook 1. Global State of the Environment Report 1997*, Oxford University Press, New York; World Bank (1992), World Development Report 1992, Washington DC.; World Resources Institute (1994), *World Resources 1994-95*, Oxford University Press, New York; World Resources Institute (1996), *World Resources 1996-97*, Oxford University Press, New York.

LIST OF FIGURES AND TABLES

Figures

Tables

INDEX

European Union
9, 12, 33, 37, 65, 91, 131

F

Financial markets
16, 18, 19, 29, 53, 54, 56, 86, 93, 104

Foreign direct investment (FDI)
9, 13, 20, 31, 38, 39, 40, 42, 43, 48, 50, 51, 52, 56, 95, 129, 130, 138

France
9, 30, 43, 81, 91, 111, 121

G

Gender issues
133

Germany
9, 30, 58, 59, 91, 111, 121

Globalisation
5, 7, 11, 12, 13, 15, 16, 17, 18, 22, 23, 24, 29, 30, 31, 36, 38, 46, 47, 55, 56, 57, 58, 60, 61, 65, 74, 93, 98, 112, 113, 114, 122, 125, 128, 129, 130, 134, 137

Greenhouse gas emissions (see also **CO₂ emissions, Greenhouse gas emissions**)
22, 60, 132

H

Health care
15, 63, 65, 96, 97, 102, 114, 133

I

Income distribution
68, 107, 111

India
9, 11, 14, 23, 30, 32, 33, 36, 39, 40, 43, 46, 58, 59, 60, 66, 70, 76, 78, 79, 80, 83, 86, 91, 107, 109, 110, 111, 115, 116, 117, 118, 119, 120, 121, 123, 126, 128, 129, 131, 134

Indonesia
9, 11, 13, 32, 36, 39, 40, 42, 43, 58, 59, 60, 66, 80, 86, 91, 107, 109, 110, 111, 118, 122, 123, 129, 134, 135

Inflation
16, 66, 109, 134

Information technology
14, 16, 45, 105

Innovation
6, 22, 37, 44, 78, 80, 81, 93, 95, 96, 120

Investment
5, 9, 10, 11, 12, 13, 16, 17, 18, 20, 22, 23, 25, 30, 31, 38, 40, 42, 43, 44, 46, 47, 48, 49, 50, 51, 52, 53, 54, 55, 56, 57, 62, 63, 65, 66, 74, 76, 79, 80, 81, 83, 86, 87, 88, 89, 93, 95, 107, 110, 111, 112, 113, 116, 117, 118, 119, 120, 125, 128, 129, 130, 131, 132, 133, 137, 138

J

Japan
3, 9, 14, 19, 30, 32, 33, 36, 37, 42, 44, 46, 58, 59, 63, 65, 74, 78, 80, 83, 91, 95, 98, 111, 121, 135

L

Labour standards
17, 48, 50

Latin America
13, 20, 30, 34, 40, 43, 44, 58, 60, 68, 78, 86, 91, 110, 111, 112, 113, 128, 134

M

Macroeconomic stability
93, 111

Mercosur
50, 128, 131

Middle East
30, 34, 66, 68, 78, 91, 94, 120, 123

Migration
65, 130, 133, 134

Multilateral Agreement on Investment (MAI)
5, 10, 54, 55, 56, 57, 128

Multilateral system
61

N

NAFTA
47, 48, 49, 50

Nuclear energy
81, 82, 132

O

Official development assistance (ODA)
40, 42, 63

P

Pensions
88, 96, 101, 102, 103, 104

Pension funds
38, 52, 130, 137

Poverty
57

Privatisation
38, 43, 133

Productivity
94, 95, 99, 101, 102, 104, 112, 116, 117, 122, 123

Protectionist pressures
14, 17

R

Regulatory reform
93, 95

Russia
107, 109, 110, 118, 120, 121, 127

S

Savings
99, 101, 104, 105, 106, 123

Services trade
37, 44, 71

SMEs
36, 42, 130

Social policy
6, 16, 19, 96, 101, 103, 105, 106, 130, 133

Sub-Saharan Africa
10, 11, 13, 23, 30, 39, 43, 66, 68, 70, 86, 107, 117, 134

Sustainable development
5, 6, 11, 21, 23, 24, 25, 114, 120, 121, 126, 127, 128, 134, 135

T

Taxation
18, 20, 24, 117, 120, 130

Technology
3, 9, 14, 16, 19, 22, 29, 35, 45, 50, 51, 57, 58, 65, 79, 80, 81, 95, 105, 107, 111, 112, 113, 118, 119, 127, 128, 130, 131, 132

Trade
3, 5, 9, 10, 11, 12, 13, 14, 15, 16, 17, 19, 20, 22, 23, 25, 29, 30, 31, 32, 33, 34, 35, 36, 37, 42, 43, 44, 45, 46, 47, 48, 49, 50, 54, 55, 57, 58, 61, 62, 65, 70, 71, 74, 76, 78, 79, 80, 93, 94, 95, 99, 104, 107, 109, 110, 112, 113, 116, 117, 119, 120, 122, 125, 126, 128, 129, 130, 131, 133, 134, 137, 138

Trade policy
129, 133

U

United Kingdom
9, 43, 91

United States
9, 15, 32, 34, 36, 37, 42, 43, 46, 58, 59, 63, 65, 78, 83, 91, 95, 111, 112, 119, 121, 130, 138

Uruguay Round
10, 16, 31, 37, 44, 45, 46, 49, 54, 55, 131, 133, 138

W

World Trade Organisation (WTO)
9, 10, 16, 17, 23, 25, 32, 33, 34, 44, 46, 47, 48, 49, 55, 125, 128, 129

MAIN SALES OUTLETS OF OECD PUBLICATIONS
PRINCIPAUX POINTS DE VENTE DES PUBLICATIONS DE L'OCDE

AUSTRALIA – AUSTRALIE
D.A. Information Services
648 Whitehorse Road, P.O.B 163
Mitcham, Victoria 3132   Tel. (03) 9210.7777
                             Fax: (03) 9210.7788

AUSTRIA – AUTRICHE
Gerold & Co.
Graben 31
Wien I   Tel. (0222) 533.50.14
                             Fax: (0222) 512.47.31.29

BELGIUM – BELGIQUE
Jean De Lannoy
Avenue du Roi, Koningslaan 202
B-1060 Bruxelles   Tel. (02) 538.51.69/538.08.41
                             Fax: (02) 538.08.41

CANADA
Renouf Publishing Company Ltd.
5369 Canotek Road
Unit 1
Ottawa, Ont. K1J 9J3   Tel. (613) 745.2665
                             Fax: (613) 745.7660

Stores:
71 1/2 Sparks Street
Ottawa, Ont. K1P 5R1   Tel. (613) 238.8985
                             Fax: (613) 238.6041

12 Adelaide Street West
Toronto, QN M5H 1L6   Tel. (416) 363.3171
                             Fax: (416) 363.5963

Les Éditions La Liberté Inc.
3020 Chemin Sainte-Foy
Sainte-Foy, PQ G1X 3V6   Tel. (418) 658.3763
                             Fax: (418) 658.3763

Federal Publications Inc.
165 University Avenue, Suite 701
Toronto, ON M5H 3B8   Tel. (416) 860.1611
                             Fax: (416) 860.1608

Les Publications Fédérales
1185 Université
Montréal, QC H3B 3A7   Tel. (514) 954.1633
                             Fax: (514) 954.1635

CHINA – CHINE
Book Dept., China National Publications
Import and Export Corporation (CNPIEC)
16 Gongti E. Road, Chaoyang District
Beijing 100020   Tel. (10) 6506-6688 Ext. 8402
                             (10) 6506-3101

CHINESE TAIPEI – TAIPEI CHINOIS
Good Faith Worldwide Int'l. Co. Ltd.
9th Floor, No. 118, Sec. 2
Chung Hsiao E. Road
Taipei   Tel. (02) 391.7396/391.7397
                             Fax: (02) 394.9176

**CZECH REPUBLIC –
RÉPUBLIQUE TCHÈQUE**
National Information Centre
NIS – prodejna
Konviktská 5
Praha 1 – 113 57   Tel. (02) 24.23.09.07
                             Fax: (02) 24.22.94.33
E-mail: nkposp@dec.niz.cz
Internet: http://www.nis.cz

DENMARK – DANEMARK
Munksgaard Book and Subscription Service
35, Nørre Søgade, P.O. Box 2148
DK-1016 København K   Tel. (33) 12.85.70
                             Fax: (33) 12.93.87

J. H. Schultz Information A/S,
Herstedvang 12,
DK – 2620 Albertslung   Tel. 43 63 23 00
                             Fax: 43 63 19 69
Internet: s-info@inet.uni-c.dk

EGYPT – ÉGYPTE
The Middle East Observer
41 Sherif Street
Cairo   Tel. (2) 392.6919
                             Fax: (2) 360.6804

FINLAND – FINLANDE
Akateeminen Kirjakauppa
Keskuskatu 1, P.O. Box 128
00100 Helsinki

Subscription Services/Agence d'abonnements :
P.O. Box 23
00100 Helsinki   Tel. (358) 9.121.4403
                             Fax: (358) 9.121.4450

*FRANCE
OECD/OCDE
Mail Orders/Commandes par correspondance :
2, rue André-Pascal
75775 Paris Cedex 16   Tel. 33 (0)1.45.24.82.00
                        Fax: 33 (0)1.49.10.42.76
                        Telex: 640048 OCDE
Internet: Compte.PUBSINQ@oecd.org

Orders via Minitel, France only/
Commandes par Minitel, France exclusivement :
36 15 OCDE

OECD Bookshop/Librairie de l'OCDE :
33, rue Octave-Feuillet
75016 Paris   Tel. 33 (0)1.45.24.81.81
                        33 (0)1.45.24.81.67

Dawson
B.P. 40
91121 Palaiseau Cedex   Tel. 01.89.10.47.00
                             Fax: 01.64.54.83.26

Documentation Française
29, quai Voltaire
75007 Paris   Tel. 01.40.15.70.00

Economica
49, rue Héricart
75015 Paris   Tel. 01.45.78.12.92
                             Fax: 01.45.75.05.67

Gibert Jeune (Droit-Économie)
6, place Saint-Michel
75006 Paris   Tel. 01.43.25.91.19

Librairie du Commerce International
10, avenue d'Iéna
75016 Paris   Tel. 01.40.73.34.60

Librairie Dunod
Université Paris-Dauphine
Place du Maréchal-de-Lattre-de-Tassigny
75016 Paris   Tel. 01.44.05.40.13

Librairie Lavoisier
11, rue Lavoisier
75008 Paris   Tel. 01.42.65.39.95

Librairie des Sciences Politiques
30, rue Saint-Guillaume
75007 Paris   Tel. 01.45.48.36.02

P.U.F.
49, boulevard Saint-Michel
75005 Paris   Tel. 01.43.25.83.40

Librairie de l'Université
12a, rue Nazareth
13100 Aix-en-Provence   Tel. 04.42.26.18.08

Documentation Française
165, rue Garibaldi
69003 Lyon   Tel. 04.78.63.32.23

Librairie Decitre
29, place Bellecour
69002 Lyon   Tel. 04.72.40.54.54

Librairie Sauramps
Le Triangle
34967 Montpellier Cedex 2   Tel. 04.67.58.85.15
                             Fax: 04.67.58.27.36

A la Sorbonne Actual
23, rue de l'Hôtel-des-Postes
06000 Nice   Tel. 04.93.13.77.75
                             Fax: 04.93.80.75.69

GERMANY – ALLEMAGNE
OECD Bonn Centre
August-Bebel-Allee 6
D-53175 Bonn   Tel. (0228) 959.120
                             Fax: (0228) 959.12.17

GREECE – GRÈCE
Librairie Kauffmann
Stadiou 28
10564 Athens   Tel. (01) 32.55.321
                             Fax: (01) 32.30.320

HONG-KONG
Swindon Book Co. Ltd.
Astoria Bldg. 3F
34 Ashley Road, Tsimshatsui
Kowloon, Hong Kong   Tel. 2376.2062
                             Fax: 2376.0685

HUNGARY – HONGRIE
Euro Info Service
Margitsziget, Európa Ház
1138 Budapest   Tel. (1) 111.60.61
                             Fax: (1) 302.50.35
E-mail: euroinfo@mail.matav.hu
Internet: http://www.euroinfo.hu//index.html

ICELAND – ISLANDE
Mál og Menning
Laugavegi 18, Pósthólf 392
121 Reykjavik   Tel. (1) 552.4240
                             Fax: (1) 562.3523

INDIA – INDE
Oxford Book and Stationery Co.
Scindia House
New Delhi 110001   Tel. (11) 331.5896/5308
                             Fax: (11) 332.2639
E-mail: oxford.publ@axcess.net.in

17 Park Street
Calcutta 700016   Tel. 240832

INDONESIA – INDONÉSIE
Pdii-Lipi
P.O. Box 4298
Jakarta 12042   Tel. (21) 573.34.67
                             Fax: (21) 573.34.67

IRELAND – IRLANDE
Government Supplies Agency
Publications Section
4/5 Harcourt Road
Dublin 2   Tel. 661.31.11
                             Fax: 475.27.60

ISRAEL – ISRAËL
Praedicta
5 Shatner Street
P.O. Box 34030
Jerusalem 91430   Tel. (2) 652.84.90/1/2
                             Fax: (2) 652.84.93

R.O.Y. International
P.O. Box 13056
Tel Aviv 61130   Tel. (3) 546 1423
                             Fax: (3) 546 1442
E-mail: royil@netvision.net.il

Palestinian Authority/Middle East:
INDEX Information Services
P.O.B. 19502
Jerusalem   Tel. (2) 627.16.34
                             Fax: (2) 627.12.19

ITALY – ITALIE
Libreria Commissionaria Sansoni
Via Duca di Calabria, 1/1
50125 Firenze   Tel. (055) 64.54.15
                             Fax: (055) 64.12.57
E-mail: licosa@ftbcc.it

Via Bartolini 29
20155 Milano   Tel. (02) 36.50.83

Editrice e Libreria Herder
Piazza Montecitorio 120
00186 Roma   Tel. 679.46.28
                             Fax: 678.47.51

Libreria Hoepli
Via Hoepli 5
20121 Milano   Tel. (02) 86.54.46
                             Fax: (02) 805.28.86

Libreria Scientifica
Dott. Lucio de Biasio 'Aeiou'
Via Coronelli, 6
20146 Milano   Tel. (02) 48.95.45.52
                                 Fax: (02) 48.95.45.48

JAPAN – JAPON
OECD Tokyo Centre
Landic Akasaka Building
2-3-4 Akasaka, Minato-ku
Tokyo 107   Tel. (81.3) 3586.2016
                                 Fax: (81.3) 3584.7929

KOREA – CORÉE
Kyobo Book Centre Co. Ltd.
P.O. Box 1658, Kwang Hwa Moon
Seoul   Tel. 730.78.91
                                 Fax: 735.00.30

MALAYSIA – MALAISIE
University of Malaya Bookshop
University of Malaya
P.O. Box 1127, Jalan Pantai Baru
59700 Kuala Lumpur
Malaysia   Tel. 756.5000/756.5425
                                 Fax: 756.3246

MEXICO – MEXIQUE
OECD Mexico Centre
Edificio INFOTEC
Av. San Fernando no. 37
Col. Toriello Guerra
Tlalpan C.P. 14050
Mexico D.F.   Tel. (525) 528.10.38
                                 Fax: (525) 606.13.07
E-mail: ocde@rtn.net.mx

NETHERLANDS – PAYS-BAS
SDU Uitgeverij Plantijnstraat
Externe Fondsen
Postbus 20014
2500 EA's-Gravenhage   Tel. (070) 37.89.880
Voor bestellingen: Fax: (070) 34.75.778

Subscription Agency/   Agence d'abonnements :
SWETS & ZEITLINGER BV
Heereweg 347B
P.O. Box 830
2160 SZ Lisse   Tel. 252.435.111
                                 Fax: 252.415.888

NEW ZEALAND –
NOUVELLE-ZÉLANDE
GPLegislation Services
P.O. Box 12418
Thorndon, Wellington   Tel. (04) 496.5655
                                 Fax: (04) 496.5698

NORWAY – NORVÈGE
NIC INFO A/S
Ostensjoveien 18
P.O. Box 6512 Etterstad
0606 Oslo   Tel. (22) 97.45.00
                                 Fax: (22) 97.45.45

PAKISTAN
Mirza Book Agency
65 Shahrah Quaid-E-Azam
Lahore 54000   Tel. (42) 735.36.01
                                 Fax: (42) 576.37.14

PHILIPPINE – PHILIPPINES
International Booksource Center Inc.
Rm 179/920 Cityland 10 Condo Tower 2
HV dela Costa Ext cor Valero St.
Makati Metro Manila   Tel. (632) 817 9676
                                 Fax: (632) 817 1741

POLAND – POLOGNE
Ars Polona
00-950 Warszawa
Krakowskie Prezdmiescie 7   Tel. (22) 264760
                                 Fax: (22) 265334

PORTUGAL
Livraria Portugal
Rua do Carmo 70-74
Apart. 2681
1200 Lisboa   Tel. (01) 347.49.82/5
                                 Fax: (01) 347.02.64

SINGAPORE – SINGAPOUR
Ashgate Publishing
Asia Pacific Pte. Ltd
Golden Wheel Building, 04-03
41, Kallang Pudding Road
Singapore 349316   Tel. 741.5166
                                 Fax: 742.9356

SPAIN – ESPAGNE
Mundi-Prensa Libros S.A.
Castelló 37, Apartado 1223
Madrid 28001   Tel. (91) 431.33.99
                                 Fax: (91) 575.39.98
E-mail: mundiprensa@tsai.es
Internet: http://www.mundiprensa.es

Mundi-Prensa Barcelona
Consell de Cent No. 391
08009 – Barcelona   Tel. (93) 488.34.92
                                 Fax: (93) 487.76.59

Libreria de la Generalitat
Palau Moja
Rambla dels Estudis, 118
08002 – Barcelona
                 (Suscripciones) Tel. (93) 318.80.12
                 (Publicaciones) Tel. (93) 302.67.23
                                 Fax: (93) 412.18.54

SRI LANKA
Centre for Policy Research
c/o Colombo Agencies Ltd.
No. 300-304, Galle Road
Colombo 3   Tel. (1) 574240, 573551-2
                                 Fax: (1) 575394, 510711

SWEDEN – SUÈDE
CE Fritzes AB
S–106 47 Stockholm   Tel. (08) 690.90.90
                                 Fax: (08) 20.50.21

For electronic publications only/
Publications électroniques seulement
STATISTICS SWEDEN
Informationsservice
S-115 81 Stockholm   Tel. 8 783 5066
                                 Fax: 8 783 4045

Subscription Agency/Agence d'abonnements :
Wennergren-Williams Info AB
P.O. Box 1305
171 25 Solna   Tel. (08) 705.97.50
                                 Fax: (08) 27.00.71

Liber distribution
Internatinal organizations
Fagerstagatan 21
S-163 52 Spanga

SWITZERLAND – SUISSE
Maditec S.A. (Books and Periodicals/Livres
et périodiques)
Chemin des Palettes 4
Case postale 266
1020 Renens VD 1   Tel. (021) 635.08.65
                                 Fax: (021) 635.07.80

Librairie Payot S.A.
4, place Pépinet
CP 3212
1002 Lausanne   Tel. (021) 320.25.11
                                 Fax: (021) 320.25.14

Librairie Unilivres
6, rue de Candolle
1205 Genève   Tel. (022) 320.26.23
                                 Fax: (022) 329.73.18

Subscription Agency/Agence d'abonnements :
Dynapresse Marketing S.A.
38, avenue Vibert
1227 Carouge   Tel. (022) 308.08.70
                                 Fax: (022) 308.07.99

See also – Voir aussi :
OECD Bonn Centre
August-Bebel-Allee 6
D-53175 Bonn (Germany)   Tel. (0228) 959.120
                                 Fax: (0228) 959.12.17

THAILAND – THAÏLANDE
Suksit Siam Co. Ltd.
113, 115 Fuang Nakhon Rd.
Opp. Wat Rajbopith
Bangkok 10200   Tel. (662) 225.9531/2
                                 Fax: (662) 222.5188

TRINIDAD & TOBAGO, CARIBBEAN
TRINITÉ-ET-TOBAGO, CARAÏBES
Systematics Studies Limited
9 Watts Street
Curepe
Trinidad & Tobago, W.I.   Tel. (1809) 645.3475
                                 Fax: (1809) 662.5654
E-mail: tobe@trinidad.net

TUNISIA – TUNISIE
Grande Librairie Spécialisée
Fendri Ali
Avenue Haffouz Imm El-Intilaka
Bloc B 1 Sfax 3000   Tel. (216-4) 296 855
                                 Fax: (216-4) 298.270

TURKEY – TURQUIE
Kültür Yayinlari Is-Türk Ltd.
Atatürk Bulvari No. 191/Kat 13
06684 Kavaklidere/Ankara
                           Tel. (312) 428.11.40 Ext. 2458
                                 Fax : (312) 417.24.90

Dolmabahce Cad. No. 29
Besiktas/Istanbul   Tel. (212) 260 7188

UNITED KINGDOM – ROYAUME-UNI
The Stationery Office Ltd.
Postal orders only:
P.O. Box 276, London SW8 5DT
Gen. enquiries   Tel. (171) 873 0011
                                 Fax: (171) 873 8463

The Stationery Office Ltd.
Postal orders only:
49 High Holborn, London WC1V 6HB

Branches at: Belfast, Birmingham, Bristol,
Edinburgh, Manchester

UNITED STATES – ÉTATS-UNIS
OECD Washington Center
2001 L Street N.W., Suite 650
Washington, D.C. 20036-4922 Tel. (202) 785.6323
                                 Fax: (202) 785.0350
Internet: washcont@oecd.org

Subscriptions to OECD periodicals may also be
placed through main subscription agencies.

Les abonnements aux publications périodiques de
l'OCDE peuvent être souscrits auprès des
principales agences d'abonnement.

Orders and inquiries from countries where Distribu-
tors have not yet been appointed should be sent to:
OECD Publications, 2, rue André-Pascal, 75775
Paris Cedex 16, France.

Les commandes provenant de pays où l'OCDE n'a
pas encore désigné de distributeur peuvent être
adressées aux Éditions de l'OCDE, 2, rue André-
Pascal, 75775 Paris Cedex 16, France.

                                          12-1996